What *Kon-Tiki* uncovered about man's mastery of the sea, *Nazca* now reveals about man's conquest of the air.

This first-hand account of an extraordinary enterprise called Project Nazca is charged with the drama of a suspense thriller. Read the fascinating story of an exploration team's efforts to reenact the past in order to amass modern proof of prehistoric man's startling technical achievement.

Threading through aviation's unrecorded past—and ancient legend—the adventurous team proves that men flew two thousand years ago—and they actually re-create the flying machines that ascended from Nazca's desert floor long ago. On these timeless parched plains, the project culminates in a daring and dazzling experiment that brings us face to face with prehistoric men of stunning sophistication and intelligence!

D1603824

NAZCA
Journey to the Sun

by Jim Woodman

A KANGAROO BOOK
PUBLISHED BY POCKET BOOKS NEW YORK

NAZCA: JOURNEY TO THE SUN

POCKET BOOK edition published February, 1977

This original POCKET BOOK edition is printed from brand-new
plates made from newly set, clear, easy-to-read type.
POCKET BOOK editions are published by
POCKET BOOKS,
a division of Simon & Schuster, Inc.,
A GULF+WESTERN COMPANY
630 Fifth Avenue,
New York, N.Y. 10020.
Trademarks registered in the United States
and other countries.

ISBN: 0-671-80895-8.
Published by POCKET BOOKS, New York, and on the
same day in Canada by Simon & Schuster of Canada, Ltd.,
Markham, Ontario.
Cover photographs by Larry Gordon.

Printed in the U.S.A.

For both Lisas, and Lara

If we are to see things in their right perspective, we need to understand the past of man as well as his present. That is why an understanding of his myths and symbols is of essential importance.

—CARL JUNG

CONTENTS

AUTHOR'S NOTE

NAZCA IS SOUTH AMERICA'S MOST PERPLEXING archeological riddle and one of the world's most beautiful works of art.

Etched upon Peru's vast, barren Nazca plains are hundreds of long, ruler-straight lines, immense geometric symbols and giant ground drawings of curious birds and animals.

Some of Nazca's unswerving lines are as narrow as donkey trails, while others are as wide as modern airport runways. Furrowed lines run for miles, scaling steep mountains, straddling wide valleys. Some lines converge; some run parallel; others stand alone. The giant ground drawings have been carved upon the rocky plains with subtle sensitivity as if fashioned by a giant abstract artist. The scale is monumental.

From the ground, Nazca is totally incomprehensible, yet from the air one gasps with astonishment—and that is what most fascinates modern man. The riddle of Nazca asks why this colossal puzzle was created over two thousand years ago if no one could have seen it? To appreciate Nazca one *must* be airborne above the plains.

11

This book is the story of an expedition that probed that riddle. Project Nazca was sponsored by the International Explorers' Society as an adventure in experimental archeology—a new field that departs from the traditional study of ancient man. Simply stated, the project's problem was to determine who had flown over Nazca centuries ago. It is unnecessary to turn to outer space as the solitary answer. It is totally unreasonable that Nazca was a prehistoric spaceport for extraterrestrial visitors. Far more acceptable is the idea that the obviously ingenious men of Nazca had learned to fly there long, long ago.

Project Nazca first researched aviation's extensive prehistory and legends and then built an ancient airship of native fabrics and fibers. The result was high adventure that culminated in the spectacular flight of Condor I by world-champion balloonist Julian Nott and myself.

The project's assessment is really yours to make as you read this book. The remarkable adventure, as I experienced it, began October 12, 1973, when the first Explorer field team flew over the plains of Nazca.

NAZCA

Journey to the Sun

1

Above the
Nazca Stars

AT DAWN OUR CESSNA-172 LIFTED OFF THE runway of Lima's modern Jorge Chavez Airport and climbed into a thick gray mist that blanketed the Peruvian coast.

In the dim glow of the instrument panel, I could barely make out the face of Ricardo, our young Peruvian pilot. He seemed unperturbed as he blindly flew us up into the dark fog that was slowly rolling in off the cold Pacific. It seemed an ominous morning to begin the adventure.

Behind us in the narrow passenger seat, photographer Larry Gordon, surrounded by equipment, was trying to load his newest camera—a Japanese 140-degree Wide-Lux that exposed two 35-mm frames simultaneously for panoramic coverage.

Our mission that morning called for the widest lens possible, for we were heading due southeast toward Peru's mysterious plains of Nazca. Our assignment for the International Explorers Society was to attempt the first interpretive color photography of the unexplained prehistoric lines and symbols drawn there upon the desert floor.

For the past year we had studied Nazca and its curious history. In the first years of the Spanish conquest, there were reports of a vast network of Inca "roads," and farmers worked their fields in the valleys beside them without question.

17

All remained quiet in Nazca until 1939, when North American agronomist Paul Kosok made a startling discovery while studying ancient irrigation methods. As Kosok charted what he believed were pre-Inca irrigation canals, he was astonished to see the survey lines in his field notebook suddenly form curious geometric symbols and recognizable animal forms.

When the Peruvian Air Force took aerial photographs above Nazca, the results were sensational. Upon 200 square miles of the plains, hundreds of "landing strip" lines and large ground drawings were found.

Aerial photograph analysis of the ground drawings showed eighteen condor-like bird drawings—the largest measuring 400 feet in length. Extraordinary trapezoids and long, needle-like triangles ran for miles. At several places the long lines met like clusters of delicate stars etched into the naked desert. A giant spider, a monkey and various curious designs covered the vast plains. Other lines had been abstracted beyond recognition. All could be appreciated only from the air.

Because many of the long prehistoric pathways and giant trapezoids most resemble modern-day airfields, speculation followed that Nazca may have been the site of ancient landing fields. In fact, the "runways" of Nazca soon became prominently featured in dozens of sensational "astro-archeology" books sold worldwide in the late 1960s. The leading popular writer of this group suggested that Nazca was a giant airfield built for and under the instructions of gods from outer space. Almost overnight Nazca became a scientific twilight zone.

We talked of these fascinating Nazca riddles as we droned on in the thick coastal fog. Our flight plan now showed us to be over the cold offshore waters.

18

Fifty miles ahead lay the port of Pisco, where we planned to take on fuel at the military airfield.

We called Pisco on the radio and asked for weather —but Pisco wasn't awake yet. We flew on in the gloomy gray sky, heading southeast at 5,000 feet. The aerial map I scanned now placed us offshore from a rugged coastline of 2,000-foot-high cliffs and immense sand dunes that rolled down into the sea. The map showed few coastal towns and no navigational aids until Pisco.

I'd questioned the wisdom of departing at all before we left Lima, but the Peruvian flight dispatchers confidently assured us we'd soon leave the fog. The Humboldt Current, they explained, runs beside the central Peruvian coast, and its cool waters create a persistent mist that covers Lima nearly half the year.

"Don't worry," the chief dispatcher had added. "You'll find the sun before Pisco and from then on you'll be clear and dry. It rains about half an hour once every two years at Nazca."

Just as I was pondering that remark, our tiny Cessna suddenly knifed out of the dark mist and into dazzling sunlight. Below, the Pacific was now brilliant and straight ahead on the bright horizon we could see the Paracas peninsula.

"That's Pisco just ahead," Ricardo announced. "Let's try to wake them up again."

This time our radio crackled a response and we were cleared to land at the military strip. We came in low over a sheltered bay where a dozen fishing boats were anchored and skimmed the edge of the adobe town before touching down on Pisco's asphalt runway.

As our tank was being topped off, we filed our flight plan with the lone controller in the two-story operations tower. We planned to fly east across ninety miles of empty desert to the Ica Valley, an oasis that lies just before the Nazca plains. From there we

19

would circle over the *pampas* and photograph as long as our fuel allowed.

We were told there was no traffic in the area, nor had there been any for six weeks. We were advised that there was a small crop-dusting strip available for emergency landings at the edge of the plains. Also, at another dirt field near the village of Nazca we could probably find fuel in an emergency.

Within half an hour we were airborne again, flying east toward the morning sun. Ahead lay the nearly vanished desert kingdoms of ancient Peru. We flew on toward mountains of shifting sand that now buried forgotten worlds and fragments of civilization. Below lay the tombs of vanished generations—countless thousands of mummified corpses lying still in the fetal pose with the sands of centuries upon them.

Within half an hour the lush Ica Valley appeared ahead like the oasis it is. From our 5,000-foot cruising altitude, we could soon see beyond Ica to where the green valley met the rust-colored plains.

"That's it," our young pilot announced almost reverently. "That's Nazca."

There on the far horizon was our destination, and as we began a gentle descent toward the great plateau we soon saw the first mysterious lines. At the very edge of the leading plateau, two long, slender triangles pointed away from the rim directly toward the vast plains ahead. They did, indeed, seem like navigational markers directing us onto an immense landing field.

We raced across the plateau rim at 1,500 feet and continued descending over the long, needle-like triangles. Ahead in an astonishing panorama lay scores of lines and giant runways. It was as if a dozen deserted airports were spread out before us. Clusters of lines linked wide, empty runways. Long, bold lines were everywhere, at many angles—crisscrossing, parallel, running to the horizon.

We leveled off at 500 feet and continued toward a distant range of purple mountains. Below, a maze of geometrically precise lines flashed under our Cessna. As we sped above Nazca, all questions were forgotten. Now there was only the thrill of discovery.

Then, suddenly, the first giant ground drawing appeared on the *pampas* floor. A 400-foot-long condor with wide open circle eyes looked up at us. It was unnerving to look down into eyes that had stared skyward for fifteen centuries.

Ricardo slowly banked the small aircraft to allow Larry several camera angles. We descended to 400 feet to inspect and photograph many of the smaller drawings—reptiles, spirals, flowers, a shark, a spider and a giant monkey. We continued circling at different levels. Long runways stretched to the horizon. Arrow-straight lines climbed over steep hills that met the bright cloudless sky.

It was all unreal. There is no similar experience in our world; no one is really prepared to comprehend these mysterious symbols. One simply stares down at the incredible maze below—an ancient art form that may be appreciated only while in flight.

We hadn't been prepared for the immenseness of Nazca. In that first hour we realized no wide-angle lens would ever capture it all. Shooting from within the Cessna became so confining that we decided to land at the emergency dirt strip and remove one of the plane's doors to get better camera angles.

Landing on the edge of Nazca was fascinating. We came in low over the plains, seemingly guided in by one of the long parallel lines that ran beside a narrow triangle pointing toward the small 1,200-foot landing strip. We touched down on the hard, rocky surface just beside a rising cliff of the Nazca tablelands.

When we cut the engine everything was absolutely silent—no wind, no welcome, no sign of life. There

21

were no buildings, no wind sock—nothing. It was as if we had landed on the moon. From the airstrip we could see green traces of the Ica Valley beginning on a range of low hills several miles away. The hot mid-morning desert air rushed into the cockpit. Our engine temperature gauge read 195 degrees.

We unhinged the right cabin door and stowed it behind the rear seat. Then we lashed Larry between the back seat braces and the wing strut, enabling him to lean and shoot well out of the cabin. He chained his Nikon to his belt and looped the Wide-Lux around his neck.

We raced the Cessna down the rocky runway, bounced into the air and climbed back up over the Nazca cliffs. Once again we began a series of lazy circles above the plains at several altitudes. The sun now burned down on Nazca and the rust-colored *pampas* of morning had turned a red-blue slate.

We took hundreds of exposures in the next hour. As Larry dangled above Nazca my job was to point out to Ricardo each area we wanted to photograph. I had the International Explorers Nazca survey map taped to the instrument panel and found it easy to orient myself with the giant ground drawings below.

Flying there that morning, looking for the next site upon the map and then flying above it was a fantastic sensation. Here we were soaring over symbols left centuries ago by some forgotten people who may have seen the world with eyes different from ours. I could not help wondering if they had created Nazca to be seen by some future flight-powered civilization—like ours.

The great lines below had escaped detection and destruction only because of their large scale. Had they been recognizable from the ground, they surely would have been mutilated through the centuries. Had they been drawn there for us? Could they hold a message

22

from some preliterate age? Were they functional or ceremonial? Questions kept coming.

There was another strange, unexplainable sensation I felt in those first hours over Nazca. It was the feeling that someone had flown here long before us. The Nazca builders would hardly have created all this splendor without being able to appreciate it—without being able to see it. I'm sure Egypt's pyramid builders could never have worked blindfolded—never having been able to stand back and admire their work. I felt the people who built Nazca had to have seen it. It is all just too incredible to have never been seen or admired by its creators.

When we had photographed the major lines and symbols, I asked Ricardo to climb to 9,000 feet. We pulled up steeply in a wide circle and watched some of the smaller lines disappear with the increased altitude. We leveled off at about 9,000 feet and circled. Below the major lines radiated from several star-like centers.

"We are above the stars now," Ricardo said. "The long lines that meet together from what we call the stars of Nazca."

"Fantastic!" was all I could offer.

"Now let me show you something more fantastic," Ricardo said as he banked the small aircraft and pointed toward the coast.

"What'd he say?" Larry called from the back.

"Load up your cameras," I translated. "He says we haven't seen anything yet."

2

Candelabra
of the Andes

OUR TINY PLANE DARTED ACROSS THE VAST Nazca desert toward the sea. Inside the cramped cabin we talked excitedly of what had just been exposed to our minds and cameras. It was more than either of us could handle.

"We'll be over the coast in twenty minutes," Ricardo advised us. "Then I'll fly you across the bay to the Candelabra. It should be magnificent in the afternoon sun. It's a perfect day for sightseeing."

We felt like lucky tourists, joyriding over the Peruvian desert, skipping from one fantastic sight to another. Nazca's future as a world-famed tourist attraction is guaranteed, and Ricardo seemed like the perfect guide as he went on explaining what we were about to see.

"The Candelabra," he began, "is really a total mystery. We don't even know if it's a candelabra, or the Trinity, or, perhaps, as some say, it may represent the tree of life. The latest guess is that it's an aerial navigation guide pointing toward the Nazca runways."

"Is it?" I interjected. "Does it point toward Nazca?"

"No. It's several degrees off on any compass reading I've ever made. If an ancient astronaut had followed the Candelabra, he would have missed Nazca by more than 150 miles."

"What is known about the Candelabra?" Larry asked.

"Not much more than you'll soon see from the air," the young Peruvian answered. "We've measured the symbol from top to bottom, and it's 840 feet high. And it's been engraved there since the earliest Spanish navigators first sighted it from the sea."

"You mean the Candelabra can be seen from the sea?" I asked.

"Yes. Unlike Nazca, which can only be appreciated from the air, the Candelabra is easily visible from the sea. However, as you'll see, it's absolutely sensational from 1,500 feet."

We continued talking of the Candelabra as we crossed the Sahara-like wasteland below. Not a tree, not a trail, not a track marred the huge golden dunes below. From here south over 1,000 miles through the vast Chilean Atacama Desert, there are many valleys where it has never rained in history.

We were flying at 4,000 feet, and as we picked up the Pacific visually on the horizon, clear air turbulence began buffeting our Cessna.

"From here on out over the Candelabra it's always rough washboard all the way," Ricardo announced. "Buckle up and hang on. It's like this every afternoon."

We flew straight into the clear, choppy air and out over the Bay of Pisco. On our left a giant rocky cliff angled toward the sea.

"That's it," Ricardo said, motioning. "When we swing around you'll see it clearly."

The little plane shuddered through a sudden updraft and we felt our stomachs sink as the plane lurched upward.

"Hang on!" Ricardo yelled as he banked into the unsettled air.

Suddenly, despite the pitching aircraft, the Candelabra was clearly visible straight ahead. The afternoon sun was slanting across the mountain, and soft, sandy shadows vividly etched the ancient design. The Candelabra of the Andes is incredible from the air.

From the open door Larry was snapping what were to be some of the most dramatic photos of his career. Later we were to spend hours studying his Wide-Lux shots of the entire Pisco peninsula, with the Candelabra dominating the huge mountain now just under our wing.

Ricardo snapped the Cessna up just above the peak. As he banked the sensation was as if our wing tip was pirouetting the Candelabra's sandy summit. Larry's automatic Nikon snapped away at each new dizzying angle. I shot black-and-white film with a second camera. For ten minutes we fought the turbulence and the dizziness that comes from looking through viewfinders at the slanting scenes.

Each pass, each new angle, each deepening shadow gave us a new view of the Candelabra. The immense, mysterious shape rose up to meet us each time we flew toward the mountain. There was no time to think of its meaning—just barely enough time to gulp the cold, rushing air from the open door, concentrate on our cameras, change exposures and to quickly load new film each time we passed over the mountaintop.

We had flown for over twenty minutes in the superb late-afternoon light. We decided on one final pass from 2,500 feet when Ricardo suddenly pulled away from the mountain.

He leaned back toward me, shouting, "Oil!"

He pointed to the oil pressure gauge—its white needle registered in the red.

Instantly we began a bumpy glide path toward the military airstrip across the bay. Halfway there—at 1,800 feet—the engine stopped and rushing wind became the only sound. Ricardo was radioing the tower about our problem, asking for immediate clearance to land.

As we descended the air became smoother and we were soon certain we had enough altitude to reach the field. Ricardo confidently approached his first dead-stick landing as we skimmed the tiny fishing village that stood before the landing strip. He nodded toward the two of us as if to say, "Relax, *gringos,* we'll make it."

And make it we did. We even rolled all the way to the small operations tower, where the lone operator ran out to meet us. The smoking Cessna braked to a stop and the three of us just sat there for a moment before we began smelling the hot, burning oil from our engine.

"If we'd had the door on, we'd have smelled the trouble earlier," Ricardo said apologetically. We began collecting our film and gear from the back seat and floor. When we stepped from the plane, we no longer felt like tourists.

Larry was green and I felt queasy. Larry sat down beside the plane with his head in his hands. The full day of flying and photographing had reached a dizzy climax in the turbulence off the Candelabra.

"My God, Ricardo!" I said. "You don't do this every day! First the Lima fog, then the Candelabra and finally the glide in here. We've been through the wringer."

"I usually don't include the Candelabra," he said, "but it may somehow be connected with Nazca, so I thought you'd want to see it. Anyway, you'll have plenty of time to get your heads and stomachs back together. This plane isn't going anywhere. You'll have to walk into Pisco and find a ride back to Lima. I'll have to stay with the plane."

We thanked the young Peruvian before we left him standing beside the still-smoking Cessna. There were no cars at the airfield, nor any in sight, so we walked down the dusty road toward the fishing village of Pisco. The sun was setting on the Pacific and a dark night was coming up fast over the desert behind us. Along the narrow road a few *cantinas* blared out wild Spanish radio music.

When we reached the wharf I began asking how to get to Lima. Here there were no taxis, no hotels, no bus stops. I thought it curious that here—beside this extraordinary mountainside—the tentacles of tourism had not yet touched. Had the Candelabra been in Italy or California, it would have been world-famous for centuries. Yet, here, in this quiet fishing village, there was not even a postcard for sale. But that is part of the fascination I have with South America today.

Finally, as always in ports the world over, we found our ride in a saloon. An ancient Studebaker pickup truck was soon leaving for Lima with a cargo of dried fish. After we'd bought a round of *pisco*, we were most welcome. Within an hour we were out upon the Pan American Highway rattling toward the Peruvian capital.

The five-hour drive went quickly, for we sat there with our minds racing with questions. The International Explorer Society was planning a field trip to Nazca, and Larry's photographs would illustrate the brochure. I was to write the copy and set up ground arrangements.

As we drove north along the stark desert coast, I began asking myself endless questions. I'd found the hours over Nazca fascinating, yet distressing, for there are so few answers to the mystery. This strange blending of primitive, yet sophisticated, art is an ancient monument that has managed to defy time; yet, it has lost its message. These curious lines, like the pyramids of ancient Egypt, were built upon the desert. Yet, instead of looking up to a towering structure, one must

31

look down from a great height upon a complex geometry. I thought back over the initial research we had done on Nazca.

The most illuminating work was written by a German-born mathematician, Maria Reiche, who since 1946 has singlehandedly worked to complete a detailed map of the Nazca lines. In 1968 she published a scientific evaluation of the Nazca mystery. Her work explained how the absence of rain plus a cushion of warm air protecting the lines from strong winds have enabled them to survive for centuries. She detailed how the ancient Nazca people had moved and piled up millions of rocks to expose the light ground underneath. She photographed, measured and charted the long lines and drawings, and she has led the drive for their protection.

Maria Reiche concluded that the authors of "these giant documents" proved the early Peruvians reached a high cultural level. The fact that they could plan and convert from one scale into another solidly demonstrated the faculty of abstract thinking. For her book she chose the title of *Mystery on the Desert*—and that is exactly what Nazca is today.

3

The Great Gatsby

OUR GROWING FASCINATION WITH NAZCA continued when we returned to the United States. Larry's dramatic photographs were sensational. He had captured the long runways and the diamond and needle-like triangle shapes that clustered together on the plains. One long photo mural beautifully scaled the Pan American Highway with a giant "runway" it bisected.

To fuel our vivid imaginations, we now had detailed color murals of the major ground drawings as well as close-ups of mysterious "burn pits" at the ends of some runways. A complete set of the International Explorers' Society's Nazca photographs were circulated to interested members with a memo attached asking for ideas.

First to respond was Michael DeBakey, the thirty-five-year-old son of the famed heart surgeon, and an Explorer director in Peru. Mike, an energetic Texan, owns and operates his own self-created Peruvian conglomerate. Included in his varied enterprises is a tour company that had just begun pioneering sightseeing flights over the Nazca plains.

"It's time someone came up with a more logical explanation of the Nazca plains," he wrote. "The majority of travelers coming to Peru are badly misinformed about Nazca. Many of them have read one or more of the "astro-archeology" books and want to go out and see the ancient spaceport. We hate to fly them out there when they're expecting to see UFO's and little green men.

"Nazca was absolutely not a spaceport for ancient astronauts," Mike continued, "and the best testimonial to that comes from Maria Reiche. As you know, she's walked miles and measured every runway out there. She claims it would be impossible for anyone to land or take off there because the soft ground simply won't support the weight of even the lightest aircraft. Maria is right when she says any spaceman landing at Nazca would have gotten stuck."

Several of us at Explorer headquarters agreed with Mike that something should be done about the wild speculation being published and popularized concerning Nazca's being an ancient spaceport. We asked Mike to check further on some of the wildest theories. Within three months he had led an I.E.S. field team to Nazca to investigate the curious burn pits for radiation and to allow geologists to analyze them.

The "pits" are one of Nazca's most perplexing puzzles. At the end of the major runways there are large circular scorched areas. Some are shallow pits and others are flat, sandy rockpiles of stones that had long ago been fired by great heat. Freewheeling "astro-archeologists" claimed these were the burn marks from prehistoric rocket exhaust.

Mike tested the pits for radiation and the result was negative. He had pit rocks analyzed and the report indicated that they had been subjected to intense fire. The pit areas were generally 30- to 50-foot-wide circles of black scorched rocks.

"The pits appear as if there were giant bonfires there long ago, more than one thousand years back," Mike wrote. "I have always thought the runways were ceremonial or processional areas—and perhaps a giant fire was part of the ritual.

36

"Maybe," he continued lightly, "it's very simple, maybe the people who picked up and moved those millions of rocks needed to keep warm. It gets cold there at night."

Mike's report also contained a rundown on conversations with Nazca's infamous *huaqueros*—the grave robbers. If anyone other than Maria Reiche had spent time in Nazca, it was the shadowy legion of locals who earn their living by looting the countless ancient graveyards that edge the plains.

"We asked over a dozen *huaqueros* if they'd ever found an ancient metal piece, any space hardware, anything curious other than textiles, pottery or adobe in the shallow graves," Mike reported. "The answer was always negative, and those of us who have walked over Nazca never saw anything to suggest mechanical flight had ever occurred at Nazca."

The Peruvian Explorers also reread much of the wild speculation concerning Nazca. Probably the most irresponsible was a cropped photograph in a best seller that showed a strange marking "very reminiscent of the aircraft parking areas in a modern airport." When viewed wholly the "airport area" was the knee joint of one of Nazca's giant bird drawings.

"It would be damned hard for any type of aircraft to take off racing around the sharp curving lines of that big bird," Mike's report concluded.

By the time we had circulated Larry's interpretive color photos and Mike's Nazca ground report, nearly a year had passed and the plains of Nazca seemed just as puzzling as they had when we first started our inquiry. The one nagging question we kept coming back to was Mike's plea for Nazca that "there should be something better to tell visitors than outer-space nonsense."

Another three months passed and nothing materialized concerning Nazca until Bill Spohrer and I flew together on a mercy flight to Central America.

I had known Bill Spohrer for fifteen years. A native Oklahoman, Fulbright scholar and military attaché in the earlier days of Vietnam, Bill was fascinated with aviation in South America. He has lived in Lima and Buenos Aires for several years and now manages TAN Airlines, which provides jet service between the U.S. and Central America.

It was five A.M. when I met Bill in TAN's cavernous hangar at Miami International Airport. Despite the hour the hangar area was jammed with trucks, stacks of supplies and aircraft. Hurricane Fifi had just slammed into the northern coast of Honduras and the wire services were already calling the killer storm the worst in Central American history.

Bill was supervising the initial mercy airlift and had asked me to join him on the first flight into beleaguered San Pedro Sula to help find out what was needed and where.

On the flight down, Bill and I began talking of the savage storm. It was depressing talk and we decided to change the subject to what the Explorers Society was investigating at Nazca.

It was a perfect place for a long talk. There were no interruptions, no telephones—just the two of us seated on the narrow jump seats. Bill asked about our photo reconnaissance flights over Nazca.

I told him of the feeling both Larry and I shared. It's the feeling most visitors who fly over Nazca have —the sensation that someone has flown there before. I explained how surveyors and engineers claim it would be virtually impossible to construct the ruler-straight lines of Nazca with such accuracy without the perspective of height. I related how we set a compass heading on one line, flew for six miles, passed over a

38

mountain range and then amazingly came out exactly on the same line.

"I know damned well someone flew at Nazca," I kept insisting. "You simply can't see anything from ground level. You can't appreciate any of it from anywhere except from above. You can't tell me the Nazca builders would have gone to the monumental efforts they did without ever being able to see it."

"You mean you think the people of ancient Nazca flew?" Bill asked.

"I'm convinced they did. Somehow ancient man learned to fly."

"Well, maybe they flew like I did last weekend," he said excitedly.

"Like you did?"

"I bought a balloon—a sport balloon—last week and I'm just receiving my pilot's license."

Suddenly the idea was there. I had felt all along the ancients could have flown. Bill's suggestion that they flew in lighter-than-air craft seemed intriguing.

"The theory of a hot-air balloon is very simple. Saturday I'll take you up to see what you think. You'll probably be the only person alive who's flown over Nazca—and gone up in a balloon. Let's see what you think after a test flight."

We were soon caught up in the rush of events on the mercy flight, and there was no more time to talk or even think of the new Nazca idea until we met a week later.

As we drove south of Miami into the wide open tomato fields and avocado orchards that border Florida's resort capital, I thought of how little I knew of balloons and ballooning.

"A balloon pilot can only control altitude," Bill explained. "A balloon goes with the wind. You can regulate rate of climb or descent—but not direction. That's why it's dangerous to fly in town. There's no telling where we'd land, and the danger of power lines is everywhere. Ballooning is for the wide open spaces."

"Nazca is the biggest wide open space I ever saw," I commented, "and there are no pre-Inca power lines."

Behind Bill's car a specially built trailer was carrying The Great Gatsby, a brand-new Raven sport balloon. The large red, white and blue nylon pile was bundled into a heavy sack, and beside it in the trailer was a 5-by-5-foot-square wicker basket that would serve as our cockpit. Curving above the upright basket was a metal brace with a pair of coil burners pointing skyward. They would supply the power source for the heat that would soon lift us into the Florida sky.

"What do you need to make a balloon?" I asked.

"Four things," Bill replied. "Textile to make the envelope or bag that traps the hot air; a power source —like fire—to heat the air inside the envelope; calm weather to allow inflation; and finally the intellect to dream up such a contraption."

"Do you think the ancient Peruvians could have had those requisites for flight?"

"I've thought about it and I do," he answered convincingly. "I lived in Peru five years and there was an Inca flying legend I kept hearing that I never understood until now. It's the story of Antarqui," he continued, "a young Inca boy who possessed the ability to fly. Legends tell how he would fly above advancing enemy troops and report their positions. I could never understand why the Incas had picked a young, small boy to be their flier—until I thought about the effect of added weight on a balloon flight."

"You mean the lighter the load the longer the flight?"

"Exactly. If the Incas had a lighter-than-air craft, they could extend its flight by keeping the payload

40

as light as possible. This morning, for example, The Great Gatsby is going to have to lift the two of us, fuel tanks, the gondola and the weight of the balloon's fabric and rigging—and that's well over 700 pounds. If we just sent up a lightweight young boy, the balloon would climb faster, higher and fly longer.

"Next time you go to Lima check the International Airport—there's a white stone statue of Antarqui in the main lobby. He's been Peru's symbol of aviation for a long time—the legend goes back well over one thousand years."

We drove south to Homestead, the small farming community south of Miami, and pulled into a wide park near the center of town.

"Here's our launch site," Bill said, pointing to a wide open playing field. "We'll inflate here and the prevailing breeze should take us across town and into the farm area, where it's safe to land. There's very little wind now. It's a perfect time to inflate."

We quickly unloaded the trailer and spread the giant balloon out upon the grassy field. It was my first contact with a balloon—and the size was impressive. The Great Gatsby measured 70 feet from the mouth of its envelope to the top of its crown. Bill circled the flat envelope, checking the lines, rigging, rip panel and maneuvering vent. Next we unloaded the gondola, inflator fan, propane tanks and assorted paraphernalia.

Inflation was soon under way, with two of our six-man ground crew holding the envelope's mouth wide open to catch the rush of crisp morning air from a noisy gasoline-powered inflator fan. As the fan pushed air into the open mouth, the pile of brightly colored nylon suddenly began to rise. The wind inflation kept on until the balloon was nearly a quarter full of fresh-blown air.

Next, Bill, who had been checking the gas lines

and propane tanks inside the gondola, stepped inside the mount, holding the balloon's twin burners. He turned on a gas valve and lit the escaping propane with a spark. Instantly there was a burst of flame directed into the balloon's mouth.

Hot air rushed into the nylon cavity and the effect was immediate. A sudden swelling began and literally lifted fabric folds from the ground. The Great Gatsby came to life before us. I was astonished at how immediate the effect of the hot air was—the balloon was suddenly immense!

As the envelope rose, Bill pointed the burners higher toward the rising mouth. Soon the fabric was off the ground and towering seven stories above us was a great, growing mass of trapped hot air. Inflation had taken less than fifteen minutes, and already a crowd of curious onlookers was forming.

"Hold her, hold all lines," Bill directed as ground crew members added their weight to the gondola and held the long lines from the balloon's crown. The Great Gatsby began straining to lift.

"Hop in!" Bill shouted above the roar of the propane burners. "Snap on your helmet. We're ready to fly."

He kept the fire directed up into the mammoth balloon above us. Just before takeoff he wanted to super-heat the mass of air that would carry us up. With a hot balloon we would rise quickly—some 8 to 10 feet per second—and quickly climb above the dangerous power lines that ringed the park.

The moment I climbed into the gondola I could feel we were ready to fly. The basket seemed to be edging off the ground only to be held back by the weight of our ground crew. The roaring twin burners kept pumping hot air into the great bag above. The Great Gatsby was clearly straining to fly.

"Ready!" Bill shouted as he signaled the ground

crew to check that no lines were tangled around someone's foot or arm.

"Let her go!"

Suddenly we were airborne with an incredibly smooth lift. One moment we were earthbound, and now suddenly we were climbing quickly, quietly, seemingly effortlessly away from the ring of friends we had just left. I couldn't believe how rapidly the mass of hot air above us was carrying us skyward.

"Three hundred feet," Bill counted.

There was a small instrument panel strapped to a corner of the basket we rode in. An altimeter was giving altitude and beside it a variometer showed our rate of climb—now 15 feet per second. We were shooting up.

"One thousand."

There were also other gauges. A pyrometer recorded air temperature at the balloon's crown—it read 250 degrees, good and hot for a high climb. On the propane tanks, the gauges read 90 percent full.

When we reached 1,500 feet, our rate of climb began to slow, and at 1,700 feet we gently stopped rising. For a few moments we floated there with the slight breeze in an incredibly free sensation of equilibrium. I had never before been aloft without the sound of powered flight or the rushing air of a soaring glider. Suddenly there we were, dangling high above the city, flowing with the wind and suspended in the air —by the air. It is a glorious feeling—that first moment of a balloon flight. We were a cloud.

"Feel like an Inca?" Bill asked.

"Call me Antarqui," I answered.

We flew for several minutes before Bill pulled the blast valve rings that forced propane-fed flames to rush up inside the balloon.

"That's how we fly," he said, demonstrating. "When she begins to cool, we put on the fire."

43

"How fast is the response?"

"Just a few seconds."

And to demonstrate we descended gradually to 1,200 feet with the variometer showing a 15-foot-per-minute descent.

Then Bill gave a blast of propane for about ten seconds. The descent stopped and we returned to equilibrium. "You'll get the hang of it quickly," Bill explained. "As long as we have heat, we have lift."

For the first time since we had lifted off the field I looked around. Hanging there silently in the sky was magnificent. Ahead lay wide open fields of the farming lands. Behind I saw the rising sun spilling the new day's light upon Key Largo twenty miles to the southeast.

This is flying, I thought, *really* flying.

We drifted with the clouds out toward avocado orchards. Below we could see people pointing and waving up to us. Every dog in town seemed to be barking.

"Dogs have an inbred terror at the sight of a large balloon," Bill said. "It seems more than a fear—I don't know why. Balloonists aren't very popular with cattlemen, either. Livestock can go berserk at the sudden sight of a balloon."

We left Homestead's howling dogs and flew on toward the open fields. It was a magnificent day to fly and the gentle wind carried us westward at a ground speed of no more than five or six miles per hour.

Below we watched our chase crew winding through the farm roads following us. We gave them directions on our walkie-talkie. It was easy for us to pick the right dirt roads for them to follow. I could see how very valuable an airborne spotter would have been to an ancient army.

During that first flight both of us kept talking of the idea that ancient man flew. We found the possibilities intriguing and decided to ask the Explorers'

Society to consider sending a research team to South America to begin investigating the possibility of lighter-than-air flight in ancient Peru.

"Let's see if the ancient Nazca really had the requisites for flight," Bill said. "What they would have needed most would have been a textile that would have held hot air."

As we talked we would slowly descend until Bill fired the burners. Then we would climb slightly before leveling off again to begin drifting on toward the west. After twenty minutes aloft we spotted a large, freshly cultivated field directly ahead.

"There's our landing field," Bill said, pointing.

We gradually slipped lower toward the inviting, freshly plowed field. Our descent rate was even and the wind was soft. From time to time Bill would open the burners for just a moment to slow our descent. At one point he pulled the line that opened the circular maneuvering vent near the balloon's crown. It allowed considerable hot air to escape and instantly accelerated our descent. We continued drifting toward the field.

The basket touched down gently and the wind seemed to die as we hit the field. The balloon rolled slowly over onto the ground and Bill pulled the red rip line that tore open the crown of the balloon and the great mass of hot air escaped. Our huge nylon bag sagged quickly and fell onto the field. The landing had been perfect. I didn't realize it then, but it was the smoothest balloon landing I would ever experience.

When the balloon was nearly flat we climbed out of the gondola, and without warning I felt a cold stream pouring over my head.

"Champagne," Bill said and laughed. "It's traditional. On your first balloon flight you get showered with champagne—and on every flight thereafter you

45

drink it. The custom began with the French, who claim to have invented ballooning, but maybe we'll change all that."

Within minutes our chase crew arrived and champagne was passed around. A startled farmer came out to see what had fallen in his field, and he soon downed a glass of champagne with us before we all rolled up the mountain of fabric and carried it back to the trailer.

"Well, what do you think?" Bill asked as we drove. "Would Nazca be spectacular from a balloon?"

"It would be fantastic—and one hell of an adventure. Let's go to Peru and begin serious research."

That called for another bottle of champagne, which was quickly passed around. I was beginning to understand the appeal of ballooning.

4

Desert Graves

AVIATION'S PREHISTORY REACHES FAR BACK INTO man's shadowy past—well beyond the limits of recorded history. Early man placed his gods in the sky and then began telling legends of their flight.

Man, of course, has watched the flight of birds since the dawn of consciousness. Primitive man lived constantly with fire and watched the magical rise of smoke into the air. From early cave drawings and pottery designs, we have learned that early man certainly had the aspiration to fly. From legends we know he had the idea of flight.

In ancient China "cloud ladders" reached into the sky carrying ancients aloft. The romantic fables of the Near East tell of countless "flying carpets"—waving slips of textile that carried man aloft. In the lore and legend of ancient America, there are scores of stories of flight.

In the early months of 1973 we began collecting these legends and myths and stories of ancient flight from all over the world. We were astonished to find such a great wealth of fascinating material. Soon, the Explorer files were bulging with clippings, books, pottery, art reproductions and Xeroxed copies of reports from every continent.

We found that the idea and concept of flying have been common to nearly every ancient culture in the world. In ancient Hindu legends the flying crafts of

the gods were called *vinamas*. In post-Vedic litera-
ture the original solar bird was named Garuda—and
Indian legends say this mythological concept stimulated
imaginations to produce ancient airships.

Chinese fables tell of the country of yü min (flying folks), who lived and flew near the sea.
Scandinavian lore claims sun chariots ascended over
Trundholm, Denmark, before the birth of Christ.
Among the massive Rhodesian ruins of Zimbabwe,
there are the "towers of the flying men." The ancient
Egyptians dreamed of a sky-traveling boat. Archytas,
in 347 B.C., constructed a wooden dove—one of the
great wonders of antiquity—and it flew suspended by
a pulley from a "hidden current of air." Leonardo
da Vinci designed a parachute. In Micronesia ancient
men caught fish offshore with the aid of kites. There
were ancient "birdmen" from Mexico to Easter Island. The list is endless.

The reason aviation's prehistory is so shrouded in
mystery and survives mainly upon legend is that
primitive man was largely unable to render an in-
telligent account of his mechanical science. The Great
Pyramids are just now beginning to show us how
amazingly sophisticated construction was in ancient
days. With many of ancient man's accomplishments
just now being realized, I wondered if it was too
much to ask if somehow early man had mastered the
simplest form of flight. Couldn't there have been
some type of craft that might have been used mil-
lennia ago to carry men into the sky?

While we were collecting aviation's prehistory, Mike
had been making arrangements for an Explorer field
trip to Nazca. He began researching ancient Peruvian
textiles and confirmed that they were outstanding, so
outstanding, in fact, that many of the most conserva-
tive archeologists used superlatives to describe the
ancient fabrics of Nazca and neighboring Paracas.

The incredibly rich anchovy banks off the Peruvian coast had made early man there an ardent fisherman. From the development of his nets came improved cotton fiber looms and, ultimately, fine weaving. Ancient Peruvian yarns are the best ever produced, and no machine yarn has yet approached their perfection. Dr. J. Alden Mason, the University of Pennsylvania Museum's distinguished curator emeritus, summed up the subject by stating that "the ancient Peruvians made finer textile products than are made today. The Peruvian woman is considered by many technical experts to have been the foremost weaver of all time."

We had seen several excellent color photographs of Nazca textiles, but we needed to examine some firsthand. I contacted Raven Industries of Sioux Falls, South Dakota, the world's largest manufacturer of modern-day balloons, and asked the requirements a textile must meet to form a balloon's envelope. Raven kindly sent back a letter detailing thread count, porosity, weight and strength. They added that their laboratory would be happy to test any Nazca textiles we could obtain.

Just after the Raven letter arrived, the Explorer Telex spelled out a message from Peru:

JUST RECEIVED SAMPLE NAZCA FABRICS FROM GRAVE SITES. MATERIAL IN EXCELLENT CONDITION DESPITE BEING OVER ONE THOUSAND YEARS OLD. SUGGEST YOU COME DOWN IMMEDIATELY FOR TALK WITH HUAQUEROS."

The next morning my wife, Lisa, and I were in Lima, examining ancient textile samples and talking to the old Peruvian who had dug them out of a grave beside the plains of Nazca. The old man had come to Lima with *huaco*s and textiles after reading in

51

the Peruvian press that Mike DeBakey was interested in Nazca textiles.

"How do you know the age of these?"

"They are from Cahuachi," he answered, "a tiny village near Nazca where archeologists have carbon-dated the pottery back more than fifteen hundred years."

The three delicate textile pieces he was selling were beautiful, tightly woven patterns of dark earth-red and deep brown. Simple geometric designs were woven into one and the other two were regular checkerboard squares of dark earth colors.

"Are there many textiles there?" I asked.

"These are very good ones," the old grave robber answered. "They are colored and have patterns."

"Is there undecorated, undyed fabric there?"

"A great deal," he answered, "but they are not worth bringing to Lima. There are thousands of ancient cemeteries around Nazca where you could dig out fabrics. But they are usually as plain as bedsheets."

I explained to the old man that I was very interested in the plain "bedsheets" he described and made arrangements to accompany him back to Nazca in the late afternoon. He agreed to show me where we could dig out fabric samples in areas that had been abandoned by the archeologists.

"All Nazca is a giant grave," he said. "There are many places beside the roads where you may see open graves. There are huge temples there beneath the sands. You may dig on my property. I assure you in half an hour you'll uncover more textiles than you can carry."

By sundown we were driving south along the coastal highway as the old man told many stories of Nazca and the countless graves that had been opened there for decades.

"There have been many finds of great value," he

related. "The pottery that has come from Nazca and Paracas is scattered throughout the world's greatest museums and private collections. In Lima there are colossal collections in both the Larco Herrea Museum and the government's National Museum of Anthropology and Archeology."

"Isn't it against the law," Lisa asked the old man, "to dig through the ruins?"

"Where I take you it will not be against the laws," he said. "You will find the plain white cotton fabrics you want among the leavings of past grave robbers. Most of the mummies were buried in funerary sacks, and they are excellent examples of Nazca fabrics. Usually when a tomb is opened the pottery—jewelry if any— and embroidered textiles are kept. The skeletons and fabric bags are usually discarded on the spot. You won't even have to dig for plain textiles."

It was nearly midnight when we arrived in Nazca. The sky was clear and there was not a whisper of wind. The long drive across the plains had gone quickly by listening to the fascinating old man's yarns of how to recognize an authentic pottery *huaco* from a fine fake (the smell), and what Nazca's lines and giant ground drawings were (he had never seen them, for he'd never been in a plane, and he doubted they existed).

We checked into the small, pleasant government Hotel Turista. The hotel is built around a garden patio and looked to be the most comfortable base camp any Explorer field trip would ever have. We left a call for seven A.M., when the old man would join us for coffee before setting out to search for ancient textiles.

By seven-thirty the three of us were driving west out of Nazca along a dusty, sandy road toward La Estaquería—the "place of stakes." I was impressed with the weather. Everything was absolutely still. There was not even a hint of breeze and the sky was cloudless—perfect conditions for flying a balloon.

The road followed a ribbon-like oasis river valley that cut between the high sandy ridges of the Nazca plains. It was much like the Rio Grande Valley outside Albuquerque, New Mexico. The high Andes were far away on the eastern horizon. We had two objectives that beautiful morning. First, we planned to stop for fabric samples beside open graves in the ancient cemeteries. Then we would continue to La Estaquería to investigate what some writers have called the "Peruvian Stonehenge." La Estaquería was reportedly a forest of ancient stakes and poles erected to form a prehistoric solar observatory.

Within ten minutes from town we reached the first excavated graves. As we drove along the dry riverbed, the old grave robber pointed out scores of pock marks on the sandy hills.

"Those graves were excavated long before I was born," he said, pointing toward a low hillside of sandy holes and depressions.

As we drove on, the sand dunes seemed to grow evenly on both sides.

"Those are temples, not sand dunes. There are man-made adobe temples beneath the sand. Over there on the right you can see the long terraces before each of the buildings. Look farther over there; you can see a corner that's been dug out. There are more open graves on top of that hill."

It was a fantastic tour! The farther we drove, the more we realized the enormous size of the ancient city. Here were the temples and homes of the Nazca builders. The sands of a thousand years now covered over their adobe world, but it was all still here, including their art out upon the plains, their buildings and their bleached and buried skeletons.

"It never rains here," our grizzled old guide continued. "In town it rains maybe fifteen minutes every two years, but out here it's never rained. I'll show you skulls with dried-up eyeballs and shriveled ears. Let's stop here. You'll find all the cloth you want right here."

And the old man was right. Just as we left the battered old truck, Lisa nearly stepped on an ancient funeral sack tied together with a brittle piece of primitive rope that many museums would treasure. The sack was empty and had probably lain in the sand for years, dropped there by a *huaquero* who had worked the hundreds of open graves that lay upon the hillside just before us.

"It's beautiful and strong!" Lisa exclaimed as she shook the sand away from the large white sack. "Is it really old?"

"Over a thousand years," the old man confirmed. "Look at that braided rope. It will snap in two."

That first funeral sack was magnificent. While the old man couldn't understand our excitement over the simple white fabric, we were thrilled. The soft, lightweight, ancient fabric resembled a modern bedsheet—it was beautifully woven, and when I put the pocket magnifier to it to examine the weave, I was astonished to see a close, even, tight pattern with threads more closely bound together than the cotton Levi's shirt I was wearing.

The sack Lisa had found measured over three feet long and one and a half feet wide. The top had been ripped away and it was empty. Nearby there were pottery shards and several tiny black corncobs. Twenty feet to the left we saw the first skull.

"That's probably the fellow who's sack you have. Looks like he came from a good family."

Our old guide picked up the white bleached skull and we were astonished at its curious shape. The jawbone and teeth were intact, but the cranium seemed to rise to a point. The skull was strangely deformed.

"The ancient Nazca thought a pointed skull was beautiful. So the children had boards strapped to their

55

foreheads and necks to force the skull to grow like this."

There was absolutely no reverence among the grave robbers for the longtime dead. As we climbed up the hill, we stepped over a dozen skulls and the old man nonchalantly poked at one or two of them with a large stick he carried. Some showed clear evidence of sophisticated trepanning.

Almost everywhere upon the sandy hill there were pieces of white cotton fabric poking through the sand. I pulled out several and shook them clean—they were still strong and white and surprisingly similar to modern textiles. I was astonished at how perfectly the dry desert had preserved them.

As we climbed the steep hills, I kept picking up bright red and maroon pottery fragments. Scattered among the sands were large and small shards that were irresistible souvenirs. Several had bits of design or curving handles. My pockets were getting heavy and my bundle of cloth larger. The old man had been right—within half an hour here we wouldn't be able to carry all we had found.

Lisa and I tried to find as many varieties of cloth as we could. There were coarse tan sacks that looked almost like today's fashionable handbags. There were thin, muslin-like yards of fabric with tufts of raw cotton sewn upon one side by thin, fine white thread. There were countless "bedsheets" and scores of light cotton fabric with lines and narrow designs embroidered upon the edges. We found no dyed or brightly embroidered pieces like the old man had shown us in Lima.

"What's the biggest piece of fabric you've ever uncovered?" I asked when we had reached the top of the hill.

"Some a little bigger than a bedsheet," he answered with a puzzled look.

"Any very large—very large pieces?"

"No," he answered, wanting to ask why, but not quite being able to because of the inborn reserve of the *mestizo*.

From the hilltop we looked out upon an incredible scene. Falling away from the crest in all directions, the landscape looked like war-scarred Vietnamese hills after saturation bombing. There were pock marks everywhere. This had evidently been a bonanza for the *huaqueros*.

"What was found here?" I asked.

"Many *huacos*," he answered, "very many, and some jade and jewelry, but mostly *huacos*."

"Are there any of them left in Nazca?"

"The museum has a few."

"How far does the old city go?" I asked, looking out toward the smooth hills and ridges.

"As far as you can see from here there are graves," he answered. "We may have dug a thousand here already, but there are ten thousand more within our sight. For miles along this old riverbed there are countless cemeteries and temples."

We continued searching the open hillside. Both Lisa and I were carrying large bundles of the ancient fabric, and all of it had been found without digging. The area was strewn with bits and pieces of the ancient Nazca world. It would have been easy to spend the day right there.

When we finally descended to the truck, we compared our treasures. We'd found ten distinctly different types of white or tan fabric. Several pieces seemed ideal material for balloon construction, and I was already looking forward to having them tested at Raven. We carefully packed the sandy fabric samples into large plastic bags that we'd brought from Miami.

The stark desert hills rolled on before us as the old man drove his antique truck down the ancient road. We wondered how many hundreds or thousands of treasures lay beneath the terraced hills.

"How do you know where to begin digging out here?" I asked the old man.

"Dig anywhere. The ancient people lived everywhere in this valley."

And we drove on for half an hour past tempting terraces of the ancient Nazca world. Since we had left Nazca, we hadn't seen a sign, a modern building, an animal—nothing but the sandy road cutting into the dry riverbed and thousands of empty graves dotting the hillside.

"Are there any graves that have recently been opened?" I asked, not really expecting an answer.

"I'll show you some near La Estaquería."

The old truck rattled on and the fine desert dust began caking in the edges of our mouths and eyes. The morning sun began to burn down on the sun-baked sand.

"There it is," the old grave robber said, pointing to a distant valley. "You can just see the stakes from here. On that hill just to the left are some graves that were opened last month."

We drove down a gentle slope toward a maze of jet-black posts that abruptly broke the desert monotony. I could see more than thirty tall posts marking the crest of a small, rounded rise on the valley floor.

Just before we reached La Estaquería, the old man suddenly braked the truck and pointed up toward one of the countless, nameless hills beside us.

"Up there are some new ones."

We quickly hiked up in the hot sand. There was no reason to see the new openings other than my growing curiosity. We again walked over bits of pottery and ancient cordage scattered on the hillside. Just before the summit I could see the new holes.

"That's a good one," the old man said, pointing ahead to a freshly opened grave.

I figured he had been in on the dig, for he had known exactly where to stop, and we reached the grave without a misstep. I looked down into the dark opening, which was framed by ancient timbers.

"They buried them upright," the old man explained, "and in the sacks you've been collecting. Usually underneath the bones are *huacos* and pottery. That's where the jewelry is. That's what we look for."

The grave before us was empty. Only the sandy walls were there. There was no broken pottery, no fabric. The footprints and freshly shoveled piles of sand told the story.

"Are there more graves near here?" I asked.

"Probably right where you're standing."

"Then why haven't they been excavated?"

"When someone needs a little money, they will be," he answered, "or maybe no one will ever dig right here. There are probably fifteen thousand more graves between here and La Estaquería."

We looked over the sands toward the black posts a mile or so away. It was a curious feeling to stand there in that ancient graveyard knowing treasures lay just beneath the sand. I had heard an archeologist once remark that Peru itself was a giant outdoor museum. It is certainly true in the Cahuachi valley beside the plains of Nazca.

Lisa picked up two more large pieces of fabric as we walked back to the truck. As we drove on toward La Estaquería, we closely examined the fine, even weave of each piece. Both seemed lightweight and strong enough to be used for a balloon envelope.

Nazca's Estaquería has been a mystery since its rediscovery a half a century ago. It was first called a wooden Stonehenge by Dr. J. Alden Mason in his classic, *The Ancient Civilizations of Peru.* There are

certainly parallels between the circles of British mega-
liths and the circles of stakes beside the Nazca plains.
The setting of the posts at Nazca and the stones in
England are both oval. Perhaps La Estaquería may be
more like the recently discovered Woodhenge—just
over a mile beyond Stonehenge. The British Woodhenge is most probably the surviving upright frame-
work of a roofed building—and that may be what
much of La Estaquería is.

We roamed over the ruin, walking the concentric
rings of circular posts and surviving stumps. We were
not prepared for serious research, and no one had
seemed to know if La Estaquería's oval plan was oriented to the solstice or what. We were like children
finding scattered pieces of a giant puzzle. How it fit
together was beyond us. As we walked among the or-
derly rows of ancient stakes, I made a mental note
that the site would be an ideal future project for the
Explorers. We didn't want to chip off any of the
posts for radio-carbon dating. We would leave that
task for an archeological team. We had come only to
explore and photograph and perhaps to pass the project on to others.

I had originally been drawn to La Estaquería by an
engraving in a Peruvian school book that showed the
site as a solar observatory. A line illustration showed
long sunset shadows falling over a restored Estaquería
and claimed the ancient Nazca used this spot for solar
calculations. It was very hard to see it all among the
posts and stumps that survive there today. The posts
themselves are very old hardwood trunks that are
called algarrobin. The ground is littered with tattered
ancient textile, skulls, bones, pottery shards and the
leavings of a great many grave-robbing expeditions.

At noon it was time for us to return to Nazca. The
sun was nearly overhead and the heat was beginning
to sear the sand. I could feel the crepe soles on my

desert boots begin to stick. We had taken photos of La Estaquería from all angles and collected more ancient fabric than we needed. Our mission was completed. As we walked away I wondered if any treasures lay under the stakes. There among the ruins it was hard to resist "grave fever."

Driving back past the ancient cities, my wife and I talked with the old man. He had watched us carefully pack the fabric samples and could contain his curiosity no longer.

"May I ask what you will do with the white cloth?"

"We will test it," I began, then suddenly decided to test his reaction to our plan. There was no reason for secrecy.

"Do you know what balloons are—not the ones children play with—but the big ones that are used for testing weather, and even larger ones that carry people?" I asked.

"Dirigibles?"

"Right," I answered, "like a large dirigible. We think the Nazca people may have flown in something like that."

He did not seem surprised and said, "I have seen dirigibles in the *ciné*. There was a movie I saw in Lima with a giant dirigible."

"Have you ever seen anything like a large balloon or dirigible on a piece of pottery or a *huaco?*" I asked, barely expecting much of an answer.

He thought for some time as we bumped slowly along in the sand and dust.

"Some years ago I found a large, beautifully polished black rock with a deeply engraved drawing upon it not far from here. It was a strange drawing. It wasn't pottery—just a stone about the size of my hand that had a deep drawing cut into it. I didn't know what it was; neither did anyone else. We called it the potato in the basket."

61

I didn't understand the connection.

"It was a great big potato," he explained, "and it was floating just above this tiny basket. It looked more like a potato than anything I could think of, but—yes —it could have looked like a dirigible."

I was astonished at his ability to connect the two and excitedly asked where the rock was now.

"I sold it in Lima several years ago with many *huacos*," he said. "That was years ago when the *huacos* sold for very little. I don't even remember whom I sold it to, but I do remember that stone. I've never seen one like it since."

Jostling along beside this man who sacked graves for a living, I felt some of the anguish the professional archeologist must feel when he comes upon a desecrated site and some of the sorrow the scholar feels when reading of the plundering of Inca gold or burning of the Mayan codex. What has been lost of our past has been immensely more than we have saved.

"Do you have any idea where I might find another potato in a basket?" I asked.

"No, I don't," he said quietly before adding, "but I have a friend who could make you one—a really good one."

"No thanks."

"Inexpensive."

"No," I said, "but could you draw what it looked like for me?"

"With much pleasure."

Later, when we sat in the hotel's delightful garden, the old man drew a crude pencil outline of the stone he had found.

"That's the dirigible," he said as he finished, and I noticed that any reference to a potato had already been discarded.

I thanked him for the drawing and paid him for his time and the gas for his old truck.

"Be sure you see Señorita Suarez at the museum," he said as he left. "She hasn't seen more *huacos* than I have, but she knows more."

After lunch I walked from the hotel up the wide main street toward Nazca's central plaza and main municipal building. There, nestled in a wing beside the library and mayor's office, was the Museo Municipal and its twenty-two-year-old curator, Julia Suarez de Varela.

Julia was one of several remarkable Nazca residents whom I met. She was born and raised in the Nazca valley, educated in Lima and had returned to her hometown to build a museum. Beginning over a year before we met, this dedicated young woman had singlehandedly catalogued and organized an exhibition of Nazca pottery in the tiny one-room museum. She had literally no operating monies or staff.

When I walked into her neat little world, I was delighted to find several display cases crammed with a magnificent collection of Nazca *huacos*. A small typewritten explanatory placard was beneath each piece. Large black-and-white murals of the Nazca ground drawings decorated the walls. Julia introduced herself and asked, to my surprise, "Are you one of the balloonists? I heard you were in Nazca. This is a very small town and news travels fast."

"Yes," I answered. "What do you think of our project?"

"I agree with you," she said enthusiastically. "I think the Nazca must have flown. I was hoping one of you would stop by. I want to show you some pottery designs."

We walked to one of the two display cases that stood against the back wall.

"These cases contain my favorites," she said proudly, "and this small dish might interest you."

She pointed to a glazed ceramic bowl that stood

63

alone on the middle shelf. It was of simple design and was decorated with bold drawings on the outside edges.

"I have always thought these round designs were flying balloons," she said, pointing to a large globe with a trailing, waving line. "And there are several more like this and others with what I've always thought were kites."

She carefully took the centuries-old dish from the case and I examined two flying "balloons" that circled the ancient ceramic. They did look like balloons trailing streamers and lines.

"The moment I heard about your idea I thought about the flying designs on our pottery. I have some shards at home I'd like to give you. They both have kites and balloons."

I was astonished at her conviction that Nazca pottery contained flight designs and very much enjoyed touring her small museum.

Later that evening when a young boy arrived at the hotel with a small parcel for me I was even more amazed. Inside were two pieces of a large ancient bowl. One was almost identical to the round balloon-like design I'd seen in the museum. The second pictured a kite-like object in flight trailing a waving line. For me both of them were treasures.

The next morning I packed the two shards between the several dozen textile samples we had taken from the Cahuachi graves. We stopped by the museum to thank Julia again, and she suggested that we study the "flying textiles" in Lima's National Museum of Anthropology and Archeology.

"You'll find large tapestries there of flying men," she said, "and they come from this area—from Nazca and Paracas."

As we drove back across the Nazca plains toward the sea, we talked excitedly of what we had just seen

64

8 mg."tar," 0.7 mg. nicotine
av. per cigarette by FTC Method.

© Lorillard 1976

KENT GOLDEN LIGHTS
ONLY 8 MG TAR.
**YET TASTES SO GOOD,
YOU WON'T BELIEVE THE NUMBERS.**

NEW!
KENT GOLDEN LIGHTS
LOWER IN TAR
THAN ALL THESE BRANDS.

Non-menthol Filter Brands	Tar	Nicotine	Non-menthol Filter Brands	Tar	Nicotine
KENT GOLDEN LIGHTS	**8 mg.**	**0.7 mg.***	RALEIGH 100's	17 mg.	1.2 mg.
MERIT	9 mg.	0.7 mg.*	MARLBORO 100's	17 mg.	1.1 mg.
VANTAGE	11 mg.	0.7 mg.	BENSON & HEDGES 100's	18 mg.	1.1 mg.
MULTIFILTER	13 mg.	0.8 mg.	VICEROY 100's	18 mg.	1.2 mg.
WINSTON LIGHTS	13 mg.	0.9 mg.	MARLBORO KING SIZE	18 mg.	1.1 mg.
MARLBORO LIGHTS	13 mg.	0.8 mg.	LARK	18 mg.	1.2 mg.
RALEIGH EXTRA MILD	14 mg.	0.9 mg.	CAMEL FILTERS	18 mg.	1.2 mg.
VICEROY EXTRA MILD	14 mg.	0.9 mg.	EVE	18 mg.	1.2 mg.
PARLIAMENT BOX	14 mg.	0.8 mg.	WINSTON 100's	18 mg.	1.2 mg.
DORAL	15 mg.	1.0 mg.	WINSTON BOX	18 mg.	1.2 mg.
PARLIAMENT KING SIZE	16 mg.	0.9 mg.	CHESTERFIELD	19 mg.	1.2 mg.
VICEROY	16 mg.	1.1 mg.	LARK 100's	19 mg.	1.2 mg.
RALEIGH	16 mg.	1.1 mg.	L&M KING SIZE	19 mg.	1.2 mg.
VIRGINIA SLIMS	16 mg.	1.0 mg.	TAREYTON 100's	19 mg.	1.4 mg.
PARLIAMENT 100's	17 mg.	1.0 mg.	WINSTON KING SIZE	19 mg.	1.3 mg.
L&M BOX	17 mg.	1.1 mg.	L&M 100's	19 mg.	1.3 mg.
SILVA THINS	17 mg.	1.3 mg.	PALL MALL 100's	19 mg.	1.4 mg.
MARLBORO BOX	17 mg.	1.0 mg.	TAREYTON	21 mg.	1.4 mg.

Source: FTC Report Apr. 1976
*By FTC Method

and found. I felt certain the textiles would meet Raven's flight requirements. The weather was ideal for lighter-than-air flight, and the intellect of the ancient Nazca continued to impress us. The more we dug into the ancient world of Nazca, the more convinced I became that flying men had lived there long, long ago.

We turned north at Pisco and followed the coastal highway straight into the *garúa*, the thick sea mist that usually blankets the central Peruvian coast. After the bright, warm sunlight of Nazca, we wondered why the Spaniards had chosen to build South America's "City of the Kings" in such a gloomy climate.

We checked into the proud old Grand Bolívar and phoned Mike DeBakey to meet us in the hotel's Colonial Bar. We ordered tall liter bottles of ice-cold Pilsner, plates of cheese and olives. The formal old bar has always been my favorite rendezvous in Lima, and as we sat there playing dice for the rounds, the dull weather outside hardly mattered. It is remarkable how easily one slips back into a city and the other life.

Mike arrived full of excitement. He had presented the International Explorers' project to the Peruvian government, and they were anxious to support us. Commandante Enrique Koch was ready to give all the aid Peru's Ministry of Tourism could offer, and Jorge Cabieses, president of AeroPeru, the national airline, pledged his support. With their help our logistical problems would be far less complicated.

The Explorers Society had also presented the government with a $1,000 donation to start a drive for increased protection of the plains. Resident archeologist Maria Reiche was determined to begin a twenty-four-hour patrol on the Pan American Highway to stop marauding tourists from driving and walking out upon the *pampas*. Mike and the Ministry of Tourism decided to couple the drive to protect Nazca with the project. It was to prove a very good idea.

Mike also brought news of a fascinating letter from Jay Hasheider, a U.S. Peace Corps volunteer in El Salvador, who had just made a lengthy study of primitive ritual smoke balloons now being used by provincial Indians throughout Central and South America. The letter detailed several tribes that still launched smoke balloons at religious festivals throughout the year. Hasheider had even discovered that the ancient Quechua Indian language of the Andes contained a word for "balloon maker." The report enthusiastically endorsed our theory that the ancient Peruvians had flown.

We reported on our success in Nazca and showed Mike several fabric samples we had found in the ancient cemeteries. I asked him to help us check out the "flying men" tapestries in Lima.

"They're in our National Museum of Anthropology and Archeology," he answered. "I've seen them and I guarantee you won't be disappointed. They certainly confirm the Nazca had the idea of flight. There are literally hundreds of men soaring. We've also located dozens of other ceramics and textiles that will fascinate you, including triangles and trapezoidal shapes rising toward the sun and symbols of heaven."

"Where do we start in Lima?" I asked.

"Tomorrow you'll spend the morning at the National Museum looking at the large Nazca and Paracas tapestries, and in the afternoon I'll have a car take you to the Larco Herrera Museum, where they have the world's largest collection of Nazca *huacos*."

The following day proved more fascinating than I had imagined. There's really no way to convey the wealth of pre-Inca art that somehow has been recovered and saved by the Peruvian government. There are hundreds of exquisite textiles from the Nazca-Paracas region, and conservatively over ten thousand *huacos* and ceramic pieces on display in Lima alone.

I was particularly impressed with the giant scenes of flying men. These were large exotic wall tapestries of loosely woven cotton. Embroidered upon them in soft, harmonious polychrome tones were scores of bird-like men soaring upon the brilliant backgrounds. The colorful flying men were sewn in bold, startling patterns and closely resembled figures I had seen on Nazca pottery.

The pottery collection at the Larco Herrera Museum is absolutely stupendous in both quality and quantity. Nazca art is so realistic that one hardly misses the fact there was no written language. Almost every scene of Nazca daily life is presented in bright and vigorous colors, including condor-like birdmen. We spent several hours roaming the narrow aisles that cut between the floor-to-ceiling shelves that hold the colossal collection.

When we thought we had seen it all, the old watchman sidled up to us surreptitiously and whispered, "Señores, do not miss the little room downstairs. There is where we have our *colección erotica.*"

The incredible fifteen-hundred-year-old X-rated show was more sensuous than all the French postcards in Paris.

At midnight we boarded our jet for Miami. Our baggage was crammed with Nazca textiles, and dozens of ancient "flying men" were on the film in our cameras. That night I left Peru with a tremendous admiration for the ingenious ancient men of Nazca and their impressive artistic achievements. It must have been men like these who founded the human race.

5

The Flying Man

PIECES OF THE INTRIGUING NAZCA PUZZLE NOW began to fill Explorer headquarters. Maps and murals of the Nazca markings papered the walls. Shelves of carousels held over two thousand slides of the plains, while tables and desks were covered with fabric samples, pottery chips and dozens of books on Latin American legends, ballooning and the prehistory of aviation.

Bill Spohrer coordinated Explorer research and was growing increasingly confident that we were on the right track.

"There are four major areas where our research clearly points toward the Nazca having the ability to fly," he explained to a newspaperman sent to investigate what we were planning. "First, there are the Nazca lines and drawings, which may be appreciated only from the air. Second are the great number of ancient flight-related legends that have survived in Latin America. All of these point toward flight and confirm that the early South Americans certainly had the idea or dream of flying. Third, there are many flight representations embroidered upon Nazca textiles and drawn upon their pottery. Finally, among today's most primitive South and Central American Indian tribes, the art of ballooning still survives. From Guatemala to northern Chile, we have found ceremonial balloons made of everything from tissue paper

71

to animal intestines. About all we lack is an eyewitness report of an Inca or pre-Inca flight."

Bill was unaware of a brief note that had just been mailed to us from North Carolina from Dodds Medock, historian of the Balloon Federation of America. Dodds knew of our project and penciled a brief note saying that somewhere he vaguely remembered seeing a postage stamp honoring a South American as the inventor of balloons.

"I think it was issued several years ago," his note ended.

The lead seemed dubious, for all our initial research had credited the discovery of ballooning to France's Montgolfier brothers, Joseph and Jacques, who made the world's first smoke-balloon ascent at Annonay in 1783. We had never seen any reference to a South American inventor of the balloon.

However, I asked I.E.S. researcher Ann Gadd to check for an old South American commemorative stamp honoring the inventor of balloons. She called the next afternoon with exciting news that initiated a worldwide historical search.

"I have your South American balloonist," she said. "His name is Bartolomeu Gusmão. I have his portrait and a drawing of his balloon."

"Fantastic!" I exclaimed. "How'd you find all that?"

"I just paid twenty-five cents for a pair of Brazilian stamps—one has his picture and the other has a balloon he flew in 1709. There's another in the series featuring a statue in his honor. They're trying to find that one now."

"Where's the statue?"

"It's probably in Brazil," she said. "The stamps are all Brazilian."

When Ann arrived at I.E.S. headquarters, she had all three stamps. A light green one featured a man's portrait, a blue one a statue and the last, a small red commemorative stamp, was a bombshell.

We could hardly believe the scene that the faded, lightly canceled stamp portrayed. In the foreground a circular white balloon was rising from the outstretched hands of a priest. Slung underneath the rising globe was a basket of what appeared to be hot coals with their smoke curling upward into the narrow mouth of a balloon. In the scene's background an aristocratic audience looked on. The small carmine stamp bore the date of August 8, 1709, and in the bottom left corner was the name Bartolomeu de Gusmão. It was a Brazilian airmail stamp issued in 1944 and valued at 1.20 *cruzieros*.

The second stamp pictured an impressive monument in honor of "Bartolomeu de Gusmão—Precursor of Aviation." The monument seemed to be in the center of a tree-ringed plaza and appeared to be of considerable size, with a statue of Gusmão standing before several plaques and scrolls. It was also an airmail stamp and was valued at 50 *reis*. This blue stamp was issued in 1929.

The third airmail stamp was a portrait of Gusmão that repeated the phrase, "Precursor of Aviation." It was valued at 2,000 *reis,* was light green and issued in 1929.

We passed the stamps around Explorer headquarters and each of us closely examined them. It was an exciting new lead that we decided to follow up immediately.

We sent a Telex to the Rio Explorer office asking for help in tracking down Bartolomeu Gusmão. Then we began rechecking our history books for any mention of his name.

Our standard references failed to mention any Brazilian balloonist. His name was missing from our oldest edition of the *Encyclopædia Britannica* and Oxford University Press's *Conquest of the Air*, nor was there any mention of him in the Field Museum's excellent *Prehistory of Aviation*. In the English language Bartolomeu drew a blank.

The following day the Telex rang with a message from Rio:

STATUE HONORING BARTOLOMEU DE GUSMAO LOCATED IN PRACA RUI BARBOSA IN SANTOS. REFERENCES HERE CREDIT HIM WITH DISCOVERY OF BALLOONING, BUT FEW DETAILS AVAILABLE.

The Telex was enough for us to make reservations for a weekend flight to São Paulo, Brazil, and within forty-eight hours Larry Gordon and I were bound for Brazil. In our hand luggage we carried notebooks, cameras and three old Brazilian commemorative stamps.

In bustling São Paulo we caught a midday minibus to Santos. After the long flight from Miami, we slept most of the way as we rode down from the highlands and east toward the Atlantic. We were both awake on the last long hill when the winding Santos channel came into sight.

Tropical Santos is Brazil's major seaport, and from the rolling hills outside the city we could see row upon row of giant coffee warehouses that edge the city's deepwater docks. Across the channel a full line of beach hotels stood like a miniature Copacabana against the silvery sea. We rode into the heart of the city to the municipal bus station.

We hadn't been able to find a city map of Santos before our departure, and we were hoping the Praça Rui Barbosa still existed. Several Brazilian cities have grown tremendously since the 1920s, and many of the old squares and plazas have fallen before the modern developers. We turned in our bus ticket to the control officer and I asked him directions.

"Rui Barbosa," he said, pointing, "is just around that corner. You're just a block away."

I thanked him and was greatly relieved that we weren't going to spend the day wandering all over this city of nearly half a million people looking for a plaza that may have been demolished a decade ago. Baggage in hand, we walked to Rui Barbosa.

When we turned the corner we were suddenly face to face with Bartolomeu de Gusmão. Before us in the center of a beautiful tree-shaded plaza stood an impressive bronze statue of the priest we had seen only on the postage stamp. Behind him rose a monument covered with engraved tablets and scrolls highlighted by a large plaque of a balloon in flight.

We crossed the street into the park-like *praça* and crossed the wide mosaic stone sidewalk that circled the statue and surrounding garden.

"Look at the old balloons," Larry said, pointing down at a series of inlaid stone designs that depicted early balloons and ancient dirigibles. "The whole plaza is a memorial to ballooning."

And it was—a stunning stone shrine to the earliest of modern man's recorded flights. We both became engrossed with scores of mosaic balloons, plaques, scrolls and the commanding statue of Gusmão himself. I couldn't understand how all this had escaped our history books and how this central square in a major Brazilian city could have so honored this almost unknown man who may have been aviation's genuine pioneer.

A dozen or more Brazilians were seated in the park enjoying the sun and the quiet Sunday afternoon. They soon grew fascinated with the two obvious *turista*s who were excitedly jumping from each new startling discovery.

"From the city of Santos to its glorious son, Father Bartolomeu Lourenco de Gusmão, the precursor of

75

aerial navigation—1685–1724," I read, translating a large Portuguese plaque below the statue.

"Presented with gratitude from the municipality of Santos and the Aeronautical Academy of Bartolomeu de Gusmão, Paris," I continued.

"Paris?" Larry echoed. "This statue was presented by an academy in Paris?"

"That's what this plaque says," I answered, thinking how extraordinary that the French—the inventors of the balloon in 1783—would help construct this memorial to a balloonist born nearly a century earlier.

Larry began to set up his camera equipment and I introduced myself to several of the Brazilians seated on the benches under the tall plaza palm trees.

"We're interested in the man this statue honors," I said. "Do you know anything else about him?"

But nobody knew anything. In fact, most were really astonished that we were so fascinated with the statue. Brazilians are by nature the friendliest people I have ever met anywhere, and after their initial amusement at such antics by Yankees, they soon became determined to help us find answers to our questions.

After considerable discussion they thought it best if we crossed the street together to find one of the priests at the small cathedral that faced the statue. We were soon on the fringe of a growing group determined to discover the distant details of Father Bartolomeu de Gusmão.

A young priest finally rescued us just as the growing crowd had decided to discuss the whole project further over draughts of *Chopp* at an outdoor café at the other end of Praça Rui Barbosa.

"He was a Jesuit," the Brazilian priest told us, "and was born and educated here in Santos. His dates are on the statue, which was erected in 1913 and created by the Italian sculptor Massa of Genoa. Have you read all the inscriptions on the monument?"

"No. There were some so high we couldn't see them."

"I'll let you have one of our ladders."

Within fifteen minutes we were back around the statue with a tall ladder, courtesy of the cathedral, and were now surrounded by half the children of Santos.

Atop the shaft there were several plaques and inscriptions. The most fascinating was a view of old Lisbon with a triangle-shaped balloon flying above the vaulted rooftops. Inscribed beside the large bas-relief scene was the inscription: "The Empire of the Skies Was Reserved for the Gods Until It Was Conquered by Man on August 8, 1709."

I copied all the monument's inscriptions and Larry photographed them from every angle. Then I made notes as Larry shot the scores of old balloons pictured in the mosaic sidewalks surrounding the monument.

Because it was Sunday we could not call upon the city hall, as the priest had suggested. We decided to leave that research for the I.E.S. team in Rio. There was really no more we could learn of Bartolomeu de Gusmão in the plaza, so we walked to a small open-air restaurant by the edge of the sea with several new friends and enjoyed *vatapa,* savory shrimp and fish mixed with palm oil and coconut milk and served over steamed rice. We washed it down with *batidas,* Brazil's fruit drink laced with potent *cachaca.* We hardly felt the sixteen-hour trip back to São Paulo and Miami.

In Miami, Project Nazca was rapidly taking shape. Bill had selected several fabric samples we'd found in the Nazca graves and was arranging for Raven Industries to examine them.

A collection of present-day ceremonial balloons had just arrived from Jay Hasheider in Central America. He forwarded to us three colorful 5-foot paper models that had been made by an Indian tribe near the Honduras border. His accompanying letter added that he was planning a trip farther into the highlands and would be gathering more samples and stories about Guatemalan balloons among the ancients.

When our Santos photographs had been processed, we made copies and immediately sent them with a memo to Explorer researcher Juaquin Medina Oviedo in Paris. Our initial objective was to track down the French group that had financed the Gusmão statue in Brazil. We had found their hero, their statue. Now we needed to find the Aeronautical Academy that honored him.

Within a week a report came back from Paris advising that the Gusmão academy no longer existed. In the 1920s the academy had maintained an office at 45 rue de l'Echiquier and a social address at 40 rue d'Enghien under the direction of the Vicomte de Faria. Both addresses were dead ends. However, a week later Juaquin found help at the French Academie des Sciences, where a bibliography existed on Bartolomeu de Gusmão.

Listed under the Brazilian priest's name was the brief description of a pamphlet published in 1917 that included "a reproduction of the celebrated aeronaut Gusmão's petition to the king of Portugal in 1709, recently recovered in the Vatican archives." The publisher was Impremeries Réunies of Lausanne, Switzerland. The author was the Vicomte de Faria.

The Swiss publishing firm was still in business, and two overseas calls confirmed that they had published the pamphlet but could no longer find a copy in Lausanne. They recommended the national library, the Schweiz Landesbibliothek in Bern, and that is where we finally met our Brazilian balloonist, Bartolomeu de Gusmão.

A week later a large, thick envelope arrived at Explorer headquarters and contained a complete Xeroxed copy of the 463-page, French-language edition of *Bartolomeu Lourenco de Gusmão—The Flying Man*. The fifty-seven-year-old work told a fascinating story of success and tragedy.

Gusmão was born in Santos, Brazil, in 1685, the son of the head surgeon of the city's jails. He was one of eighteen children and displayed a keen intellect at an early age. His godfather was the noted Jesuit scholar Alexandre de Gusmão, and with his support the youngster was educated by the Jesuit fathers in Santos and completed studies at the Jesuit seminary in Belem, Brazil.

In the mid-1500s and 1600s, Santos and Belem were bases for Jesuit exploration. From these Brazilian ports, scores of indomitable Jesuits were sent overland to explore the newly discovered South American continent. Many of Gusmão's teachers were men who had trekked from Santos to what is now Paraguay, Argentina, Chile, Peru and Bolivia. What they found and what they learned were taught at the famed Jesuit seminaries of Brazil.

Gusmão's formal education was completed when he was twenty-one. He was fluent in French, Italian, Latin, Greek and Hebrew, and he excelled in physics and mathematics.

The young Brazilian priest next surfaced in Lisbon in April, 1709, when he petitioned John V, king of Portugal, for a patent on a proposed "flying machine." The patent was granted and with it came a command to demonstrate the invention before the royal court.

On August 8, 1709, Gusmão appeared before the king with a small model balloon. The envelope was made of cotton and strong paper and below it was slung a woven basket of light reed. Before the assembled court, Gusmão ignited a fire inside the small basket and the curious object ascended from his hands. This was the scene we had seen depicted on the Brazilian postage stamp.

In his petition to the king, Gusmão had described the advantages Portugal would enjoy with a machine that could fly: "It would aid besieged cities, discover new regions of the globe, avoid disasters and shipwrecks, transmit merchants' letters rapidly and supply armies." The king was evidently impressed with the demonstration and Gusmão was commissioned to construct a model that would transport a man.

He quickly went to work and built a large smoke-powered balloon nicknamed La Passarola (The Sparrow). Gusmão was highly secretive about the balloon's construction and he jealously guarded his secret of flight. He alluded to mysterious metal spheres that attracted strips of iron embedded in the woven wicker of his gondola. Gusmão ended his patent petition by saying, "Please your majesty to grant to the petitioner a privilege so that none other shall dare to use this machine."

Gusmão's Sparrow was finished in October, and according to a variety of eyewitness reports, on at least one of three attempts he flew to a height of 60 feet above Lisbon and traveled just over a kilometer. His route was between the fortress of St. George and the House of India. It was, according to the Vatican archives, man's first ascent, and the people of Lisbon named Gusmão Voador—The Flying Man.

The Brazilian, however, was sadly a man before his time. Soon after his manned flight, intrigues quickly developed against him and the man and his invention slipped suddenly away. The pamphlet ends with a note of Gusmão's impending arrest by the Tribunal of the Inquisition and his ultimate death as a refugee in Toledo, Spain, in 1724. The Flying Man died in poverty at the age of thirty-eight.

Later that week two books arrived from Rio—both were thick volumes on Gusmão's life and accomplishments. Both books were published in French in Switzerland in the early 1900s and were compendiums of essays, reviews, speeches and research into the Brazilian's early balloon flights in Lisbon.

Both books included detailed descriptions of the aerostat Gusmão flew. The craft's most complete description was included in a University of Lisbon manuscript that stated Gusmão's craft "was the form of a triangular pyramid." The paper continued to describe the "skiff" as a "lightweight wooden boat that was slung below the envelope." Several additional essays described the Brazilian's flying craft as an "irregular pyramid or tetrahedron." The Lisbon report concluded that Gusmão's craft was "essentially a balloon filled with hot air."

There were several sketches of the craft and even a copy of a medal struck in Paris to honor the bicentennial of the flight in 1909. The Gusmão Aeronautical Society had also placed commemorative plaques in Lisbon to mark the flight path and in Toledo, Spain, to mark the Jesuit's grave.

The best representation of Gusmão's actual flight is reproduced upon the statue in Santos and on the commemorative medal struck in his honor. Both show a pyramid-shaped envelope with the apex upward. Beneath, suspended by lines from the three corners, was the boat-shaped gondola, which was fitted at the rear with a rudder shaped like a bird's wing. Gusmão is shown standing at the rudder, apparently operating it by hand. The medal shows the flight taking place at dawn—for the sun is just breaking over distant mountains.

When several of us had finished studying the Gusmão books, we were even more confident ancient man had flown. We were fascinated with this enterprising South American who had boldly invaded a European court with a smoke balloon decades before the French discovery. Gusmão built his aerostat of cotton and wood and flew with the heat of fire. It was what the Inca legends had already told us.

6
Condor I

IN THE LATE FALL OF 1974, BILL AND I DE-cided it was time to begin designing the primitive airship we planned to fly over the plains of Nazca. Our year of research had convinced us ancient man had flown and that the early Nazca had possessed all the requirements for lighter-than-air flight.

Our research had become an inverted pyramid. The ancient textiles, pottery, legends, myths and the Nazca lines and drawings themselves all led to a new and ever-increasing collection of artifacts and aviation articles. It was time to stop digging and start design-ing. Our homework had given us confidence—now we wanted to fly.

Our next destination was Sioux Falls, South Da-kota, and Raven Industries, the world's largest builder of modern balloons. Our first contacts with Raven had been very encouraging. They were keenly interested in our project and President Dave Christensen had assured us his firm would cooperate in designing a primitive aerostat.

I felt Raven's technology would be a great help, for the company had pioneered, designed and built a great many types of lighter-than-air craft, including NASA weather and reconnaissance balloons, giant industrial aerostats used to haul immense loads of timber, plus a line of sport balloons sold worldwide.

Also, the first balloon Bill and I had flown—The Great Gatsby—had been a Raven creation.

We called Sioux Falls and made an appointment to meet Raven's two top engineers, Ken TeKrony and Jim Winkler. On March 3, Bill and I flew north to South Dakota, our briefcases crammed with Nazca textiles, native ropes, reeds and grasses. We carried notebooks filled with drawings and photographs of early Nazca art, French smoke balloons, Xeroxed portions of Gusmão's story and several Polaroid shots of primitive smoke balloons that survive in South America today.

When we arrived at Raven's modern plant, our ancient relics suddenly seemed out of place. Here, in a complex of space-age labs and assembly-line production, we were unpacking pottery shards and fifteen-hundred-year-old textiles. We displayed our ancient collection in Raven's modern conference room and felt somewhat awkward waiting for the engineers to appear. The moment they walked in, however, that feeling vanished. Both men were instantly fascinated with what we had brought.

Ken TeKrony had been selected to help as project engineer, and Jim Winkler, Raven's Engineering Division vice president, would act as consultant. Both men were veteran aeronautical engineers and specialists in lighter-than-air flight.

Bill and I had assembled an informal slide presentation of what we had discovered and how we related it all to the possibility of ancient flight. When we had finished I turned up the lights.

"What do you think?" I asked the engineers. "Can we build an aerostat from Nazca textiles and fibers?"

"If the Nazca did," Ken answered, "I'm sure you can. We can get a quick confirmation from our textile lab. If you're ready, let's start right now."

There were two critical tests for the Nazca fabric.

To construct a balloon envelope from cotton, the material must have sufficient strength and not too much porosity. Both of these vital characteristics depend upon the quality of the material itself plus the textile's weave and weight.

We had selected six textile samples to test. Four were pieces of white fabric from the Cahuachi graves, and two were dyed ceremonial fabrics that the *huaqueros* had found in the Nazca valley.

Raven lab technician Duane Coatsworth first put two of our most promising samples under an Anchor Optical Textile Microscope to determine thread count. As he peered into the microscope, he was astonished at the dense weave and fineness of work.

"That's a much tighter weave than present-day parachute material," he said. "Our sport balloons don't exceed 160 by 90 threads per square inch. This Nazca sample is 185 by 95 threads per square inch—ideal for a balloon."

We continued testing the remaining ancient samples. They all met flight requirements and continued to astound the lab technicians. One of the dyed pieces counted out 205 by 110 threads per square inch. Present-day Peruvian yarns don't usually go higher than 150 by 90.

Next we moved to an Instrow Fabric Tester, an intricate device that tests tensile strength. One by one we locked the fifteen-hundred-year-old cloth patches in the test plate, and each time the fabric passed. The fabric was next weighed and, although heavy— averaging 5.3 ounces per square yard—it passed.

The final hurdle was porosity. Raven's Frazier-513 Permeability Tester was basically a device that measured the velocity of a jet of air before and after it passed through the fabric. A tape spelled out the findings: Orifice 6—Reading 5.7—CFM 60.5. The result on the testing data sheet confirmed that "the porosity of these fabrics is equal to or better than is commonly used in today's personnel parachute."

As the technicians wrote up the test results, we adjourned to a conference room and passed around more of the artifacts and photographs of our recent findings in Peru. Both engineers quickly absorbed our story.

When we had finished explaining the background, I asked Ken point-blank, "Can we fly with the materials they had at Nazca?"

"Yes," he answered quickly. "If they had these textiles two thousand years ago, then I'm sure they could have flown. Did you find rope, cordage?"

"Yes," Bill said, unpacking a box with ancient rope samples.

"What about the gondola?" Ken asked. "Have you thought about that?"

And with that question we began the design of Condor I. We spent the afternoon discussing basic design of the envelope and gondola. The inspiration for shape was there on the ancient pottery and textiles and the tetrahedron Gusmão had built. The size would depend solely on the amount of payload we hoped to carry.

"How much do you want to lift?" Ken asked.

"Most legends say the Incas flew to the sun—and we assume they flew alone. Some legends say the Incas were sent to the sun after death—a rising funeral pyre, a chariot to the sun. The Antarqui legend says the Incas used a small boy to fly, which means they were well aware of the importance of payload and lift. We estimate most representations of Antarqui make him no more than an 80-pound boy. His weight plus a light reed gondola wouldn't make much of a payload."

"Have you thought about a flight profile—how long and how far do you want to fly?"

NAZCA

Journey to the Sun

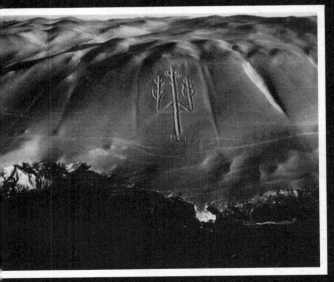

The "candelabra of the Andes" as seen from a plane over the
Pacific. This mysterious symbol measures 840 feet in height.

Views of Nazca drawings.

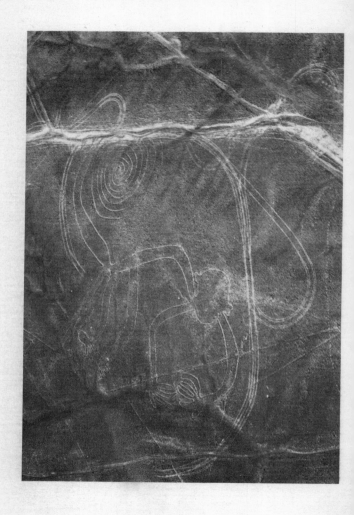

A drawing of a giant bird as seen from ground level.

A piece of ancient fabric recovered from the graveyard beside Nazca's mysterious *Estaquería* (in
background).

"The Flying Man"—Bartolomeu de Gusmao—as portrayed by a statue in the plaza named in his honor in Santos, Brazil.

Antarqui, the fabled "Inca Flying Boy," shown in a mosaic of ancient Peruvian pottery shards.

The approach to the Nazca runway as seen—naturally—from the air.

A giant hummingbird at Nazca, as seen from fifteen hundred feet up. This drawing has been carved into a plateau on the edge of the Nazca plains.

The Nazca condor symbol was painted on the Explorer research team's giant balloon by project artist Tommy Thompson.

The reed gondola for the Explorers' Nazca balloon is shown off by the old man who built it from the *totora* reed of Lake Titicaca.

Launch support poles go up as the Explorer team's ground crew
prepares the takeoff site for the Nazca balloon.

The high fabric walls of the Condor I balloon are checked to see how the smoke is sealing the cloth.

MEMBERS OF THE TEAM

"Doc" Crane,
Launch Director.

Ken TeKrony,
Engineer.

Guillermo Elias,
Nazca Coordinator.

Wild winds sweep the giant Condor I balloon from its lines in the early stages of inflation.

Left: Sudden gusting winds strike the fully inflated balloon, and the crew works frantically to keep it tethered. *Right:* Aloft in the balloon at last, the balloonists quickly tie their safety harness ropes.

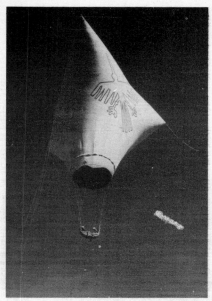

Left: The Condor I soars over Nazca, re-creating the fantastic flights of the ancient Peruvians. *Below:* The Condor I ascends to nearly four hundred feet above the Nazca plain.

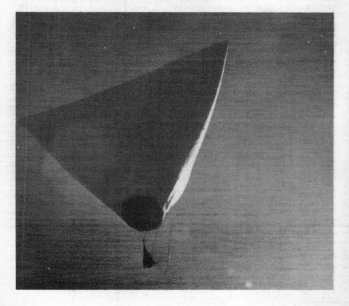

Maria Reiche discusses the flight moments after landing with the balloonists—Julian (right) and the author.

The balloonists check the reed gondola, which absorbed the landing beautifully—only a few reeds were smashed on impact with the ground.

"No. We were hoping the textiles would pass the test and then we had planned to ask your advice on design and size. Both Bill and I would like to fly. Our combined weight is 340 pounds, and we'd like to fly high enough to see the ancient runways and ground drawings, yet land safely. Our objective is to demonstrate that the Nazca fliers could have lifted off the *pampas* on a journey to the sun."

"Do the stories say they kept going?" Ken asked.

"Yes."

"They probably did," Ken answered. "Are you familiar with solar gain?"

"No."

"Well, the people you think may have flown at Nazca could have discovered what we now call solar gain. Research and experimental flights have now established that a hot-air balloon can fly by the heat of the sun alone."

"You mean we could make a ceremonial flight toward the sun by the heat of the sun?"

"It could be done easily. If we built you a balloon large enough to carry both of you, then it would approach the size that could fly on solar gain under the right conditions."

Ken went on to explain that a large envelope of hot air rising in bright sunlight reaches a point where the effect of solar heat begins to warm the air inside the balloon faster than it cools. When that happens the balloon continues to rise due to solar gain.

"That could be disastrous," Bill added. "Would the balloon we need be large enough to be affected by sunlight?"

"If we keep the fabric white or natural color, I don't think there will be any danger. We'll also design the flight profile to fly heavy—at least heavier than any solar gain could lift. I think it will be an advantage to have a two-man crew."

"What you're saying, Ken," I interjected, "is that the Incas could have flown dark-colored balloons, starting them with fire, and as they climbed solar gain would take over and they would climb and fly a very, very long way."

"If your climatology books are right," Ken answered, "a giant smoke-powered balloon lifting off Nazca could climb to 5,000 feet and then solar gain could take it out of sight. The prevailing winds could eventually carry it out over the Pacific, where it would cool off and descend at sunset."

"That would have been a flight to the sun for anyone observing at Nazca," I added. "The balloon would probably have come down in the Pacific. The dead Inca riding it would have appeared to return to the sun."

"Isn't that what your legends say?"

We discussed the legends and finally agreed it would be best to design an aerostat that would lift two of us high over the plains, yet stay below the size and altitude limits of solar gain. We were confident the ancients used balloons on ceremonial flights and that we could safely reconstruct an ancient takeoff.

In the end we decided our point would be made by demonstrating that, with fire and the materials at hand, the ancient Nazca could have flown high enough to appreciate the great ground drawings on the *pampas*.

On that cold afternoon in South Dakota our next decision was to construct a tetrahedron-shaped balloon. We took the form from both pottery and textile representations and the pyramid tetrahedron of Gusmão.

"I'm sure the earliest balloons were tetrahedrons," Ken said. "In fact, when we were experimenting with our first sport balloons, we used that shape. A tetrahedron is a simple four-sided figure—each side is an equilateral triangle. It's the simplest shape to construct, easy to sew and requires no shaped gores.

"Also," the engineer continued, "I was fascinated by the spiral designs you showed on the plains. That's the key to building a tetrahedron. To sew one you simply take a long roll of material and stitch it in one continuous spiral seam. In other words, we form a cylinder without top or bottom by sewing the fabric in a vertical spiral pattern as it comes off the roll. Then we sew the top shut—just like a pillowcase. The bottom hem is then oriented ninety degrees toward the top. To make the balloon's mouth, you simply select one of the tetrahedron's points and cut it off sufficiently for the size opening you want."

I had researched the spiral symbol almost to the point where I could argue that a spiral symbolized everything from animal's intestines to the concept of the earth's rotation. Spirals are one of the essential motifs of prehistoric art all over the world. Spirals have been analyzed and classified by size, location and direction—a creative spiral is clockwise and a destructive spiral twirls around to the left. In the end I decided Nazca's spirals could be simply a decorative motif.

Ken's suggestion that the spiral could be an ancient blueprint for the construction of a tetrahedron balloon was especially intriguing for two reasons. First, there are spiral designs at the base of several runway areas. Second, there is a long "needle-and-yarn spiral" at the very edge of the Nazca valley.

On our first flight above Nazca, our bush pilot had pointed out what he called the "needle-and-yarn" ground drawing—a faint spiral that extended its curling line into the eye of a long needle that bisected the spiral. It appears like a long knitting needle stuck into a ball of yarn, only the needle has an eye that is threaded by a line from the spiral.

91

The "needle-and-yarn" drawing is so old that it has become faint, and even with late-afternoon shadows it does not photograph well. At 1,000 feet it is, however, still distinct to the naked eye. Its new meaning became tantalizing as we talked and began making drawings of our primitive airship.

Ken sketched a crude tetrahedron shape and Jim Winkler began calculating the necessary size to lift a payload that would probably be close to 1,000 pounds. At that stage the lab technicians came in and confirmed the ancient fabrics had met all requirements for flight.

"Where can we best duplicate the ancient cotton's weight, weave and porosity?" I asked.

"We'll start checking immediately. I think we can match its characteristics, but not its quality. Those are some fantastic weaves you have there."

Raven agreed to check existing cotton samples worldwide to attempt to closely match the Nazca fabric. They would also provide the design and major assembly of the envelope. The majority of the more than 3,000 feet of seams would be machine sewn; the critical ones near the mouth and gondola lines would be finished by hand. No stitching or weaving would exceed what the ancient Nazca could have sewn.

"Don't worry," Ken said, "our present commercial machinery can't match the Nazca work. If anything, our weave will be inferior."

At that meeting we also agreed to construct the gondola from totora reed—the wild, grassy water weed the Inca used to fashion his boats. The design was taken from pottery drawings and the surviving reed boats in Lake Titicaca. Ken would give us maximum weight and size for the gondola when they had computed the envelope size.

"What do you call this airship?" Ken asked.

"Condor I," Bill replied. "Ever since we flew at

Nazca, we have been up among the condors there. I think they were another inspiration for the early Nazca men to fly. Today they still soar over Nazca, and several stylized drawings upon the *pampas* represent the ancient condor."

"Condor I it is," Ken agreed. "I only hope we don't have to build Condor II and III and IV."

"Why would we?" I asked, not really wanting to hear the answer.

"Well," Jim Winkler answered, "no one has built anything like this for a long, long time. I don't think we'll have too much difficulty constructing it once we've found the right cotton fabric; it's inflation that we'll have to start thinking about. If the Inca flew by fire, I'm sure he might have burned up his first few attempts. Also, you're going to have to learn how to fly what we build—and that may be tricky."

With those sobering notes we packed up our fancy new briefcases filled with ancient materials and headed back to Explorer headquarters. We flew back across the Midwestern states talking of how we would learn to fly a ten-story mountain of smoke and cotton across the Nazca *pampas*.

Later that week a letter arrived from Raven advising us that the design of Condor I was under way, and attached was a rather gloomy form for our signatures. It was an accident release that read in part: "The undersigned acknowledge the use of the experimental balloon for manned flight is extremely dangerous and voluntarily and knowingly assume all risks."

"What do you think of that?" Bill asked as he signed.

"I think it's time we called Lloyd's of London. I have a feeling we're going to need insurance."

7

Island of the Sun

CONDOR I TOOK SHAPE RAPIDLY ON RAVEN's
drawing boards. Initial calculations demanded a balloon of at least 80,000 cubic feet. Translated into a
tetrahedron shape, that meant a towering triangle 80
feet tall and 80 feet wide between the craft's three
pointed ears. Slung 20 feet beneath this cavernous cotton canopy would be a two-man reed gondola measuring 5 feet high and 8 feet long.

By mid-January, 1975, Raven had the initial engineering sketches ready for approval. The design
matched the triangular shapes drawn on the Nazca
plains and engraved and embroidered on Peruvian
pottery and textiles. We told the Raven designers that
no metal fastenings, wires or modern-day plastics
could be used in Condor I's construction—and they
met our specifications right down to the interface between the balloon and gondola.

Ken TeKrony designed an ingenious fastening for
the reed gondola. Four hardwood dowels would slip
through loops from the envelope and gondola lines.
All main lines would be 5,000-pound-test—five times
the strength that should be needed—and four of them
would be braided into the sixteen main lines that were
sewn into the envelope's fabric that ran to the crown.

By late February Raven had located a cotton fabric
nearly identical to textiles we had taken from the
Nazca graves. The natural white fabric had a thread

97

count of 68 by 72 and an air porosity reading of 48 cubic feet per minute. The cloth had been woven into 72-inch-wide rolls. The fabric was practically a duplicate of the ancient textile, but it had two dangerous qualities. First, it was very heavy by modern-day ballooning standards—5.3 ounces per square yard, which would weigh just under 600 pounds for the size balloon we needed. Secondly, it was highly flammable. We lit a sample patch with a match and it ignited instantly and burned quickly.

The cotton fabric was shipped to South Dakota and Raven began the initial spiral stitching. The gondola's design and construction had been left to me. Raven asked that it weigh no more than 125 pounds and be evenly balanced between two load points. They also suggested that two 30-foot lengths of 5,000-pound-test rope be woven into the body.

For centuries balloon gondolas have been woven baskets made of wicker—a material that successfully helps to absorb the impact of vertical speed landings. After thoroughly researching Inca boats and baskets, it became obvious that the most promising natural material for constructing our flying boat or gondola was totora reed, which grows abundantly in Peru. Ancient pottery shows Inca boats woven of the tubular dry reed, and the design, construction and use of reed boats has survived until today. The most famous reed boat of our time was Thor Heyerdahl's *Ra*, which was woven by Indians from Lake Titicaca, on the Peru-Bolivia border.

I asked Mike DeBakey to check where the reed weavers lived and worked, and he soon Teletyped that the ancient art was still alive on several tiny islands in Lake Titicaca.

In early April I filled a flight bag with my usual curious assortment of engineering drawings, slides of ancient Peruvian reed boats and pottery shards and flew to La Paz, Bolivia, the nearest city to Lake Titi-caca. Waiting for me at 13,355-foot-high El Alto, the world's highest airport, was our Bolivian-based Explorer representative, Darius Morgan.

Darius Morgan is a legend throughout the high Andes. A Frenchman by birth and Bolivian by passport, he has alternately been a gold miner, actor, white hunter and adventurer throughout the Amazon basin. For the past ten years he has almost singlehandedly created a modern tourism industry for Bolivia. Morgan's most innovative venture is his fleet of sleek hydrofoils that now link Bolivia and Peru across Titi-caca—the world's highest navigable lake. He, probably better than any man alive, knows the Andes, nearby Yungas and Chaco wilderness areas.

Just after landing I felt a bit lightheaded in the crisp, rarified air of La Paz. As we drove down into the canyon that is La Paz, we talked over Project Nazca. Darius had already been briefed on what we were doing, and he asked me several specific questions on size and weight of the gondola.

Within twenty minutes we were comfortably seated in the Libertadora Hotel lobby. On Darius's advice I was sipping *coca*, a bittersweet tea made of cocaine leaves that helps one adapt to the high altitude.

"I've found the right man for you," Darius reported, "He's the acknowledged old master of the totora weavers."

"Is he willing to help us?"

"I told him we were planning to build a flying boat that would go to the sun," Darius answered, "and the old man told me there are many stories of his ancestors flying to the sun. He would be honored to help."

"Where does he live?"

"I'll take you there tomorrow," he said, "the boat builders live on the Island of the Sun."

Despite the hour, the altitude and my jet lag, Darius

insisted I accompany him to a nearby *peña*, where a group of young Bolivians was presenting a night of legendary Bolivian song and dance.

"I want you to hear the world's oldest song," my enthusiastic host explained. "It will have special significance for you."

We crossed half a dozen narrow cobblestone streets before we heard the music. It sounded much like native music I have often heard in these mountains— drums, rhythm instruments and high-pitched flutes whistling strange, haunting melodies.

Inside, on the small stage of the packed *peña*, a band of brightly costumed Bolivians was dancing the ancient steps of the Andes. Behind them minor-keyed flutes rose above drums and tiny stringed instruments. The dancers were lit only by hanging gas lamps and candles upon the tables; their shadows danced on thatched walls. We had watched several rollicking numbers before a strangely familiar melody began drifting softly across the stage. It began as low, mellow, mystical music from a single bamboo flute. Soon the room was enraptured with the young Indian artist who now played with increasing intensity.

"El Condor Pasa."

Darius nodded and soon all of us were swept up into the familiar music. The flutist was now joined by dancers and drums as the condor music continued. When it ended there was an instant eruption of wild applause followed by a rousing rendition of "Bolivia." The audience sang along with the Indians. There were shouts for music of Taquiari, Yaravi and Huayno, but in the end they all sang "Viva Mi Patria Bolivia." We all sang it again before the musicians paraded down into the audience and nearly everyone followed them on out through the front doorway and down the steep cobblestone street. We watched the parade vanish from sight and soon even the sound was gone.

" 'El Condor Pasa' may be the oldest melody in the world," Darius said as we walked toward my hotel. "It probably came from the Tiahuanaco civilization at the edge of the lake. We will go there tomorrow."

"How do you know the condor music is so ancient?"

"There was an extensive study made here a few years ago," Darius said, "that claimed to have traced the melody back to Tiahuanaco—and that goes back conservatively three thousand years. They also told me that condor is a Quechua word. Few words from the Andes have entered any modern languages, but condor has, and it's a good choice for the name of your balloon. Later this week I'll introduce you to the condor men of Tiahuanaco. They may well have flown before your Nazca balloonists."

At six-thirty the next morning we were already on the high, dusty road driving toward Lake Titicaca. The early morning drive out across Bolivia's stark *altiplano* is an experience in itself. We drove for nearly two hours beside a spectacular row of snow-capped peaks glistening in the bright morning sun. Our first view of the 3,500-square-mile legendary lake came atop a small hill covered with giant Eucalyptus trees. We drove on toward the tiny village of Huatajata, a neat collection of adobe homes at the water's edge.

From Huatajata the bright red-and-white hydrofoils Darius has brought to Titicaca leave on scheduled crossings to the Peruvian side. As we approached, one of his flying boats was racing away toward the tiny islands far out upon the silvery horizon. As we drove beside the lake, Darius pointed to several small silhouetted boats offshore.

"There are your totora boats," he said. "They were building them here long before Christ. You'll be able to get some good photographs of them out on the lake."

When we reached the lake's edge, I could see the

101

ancient boats clearly. They were the same graceful, curving skiffs we had seen on the ancient textiles. Here, upon the brilliant, blue waters of Titicaca, they still survive.

"That's exactly what we want," I said eagerly. "We don't need any blueprints; all we need to do is weave our rigging ropes inside a boat like that. When can we get started?"

"Relax," Darius answered. "These boats have been here over three thousand years. I think we can afford a few minutes for breakfast first. You North Americans must learn how to relax."

Over steaming coffee, freshly baked bread and native cheese we talked of rapid changes that were just now reaching Lake Titicaca.

"In the next generation the reed boats will be gone," Darius lamented. "Everyone now prefers Fiberglas and an outboard. Only the oldest men still know how to fashion the reed. The man who will help you is eighty-five."

We talked of the lake and its countless mysteries and legends. Darius had literally explored Titicaca inside and out. He had accompanied fellow countryman Jacques Cousteau, diving into the lake's uncharted, unfathomed depths. To select bases for his hydrofoil fleet, Darius had circled Titicaca many times by land and investigated all the islands.

"When you've finished flying your balloon, come back here and I'll show you an unknown, ancient world to explore. Lake Titicaca may well have been where civilization began. There are many legends there of flying. The most popular is of the goddess Orejona, whom the ancient traditions say landed at Tiahuanaco. Do you suppose she came from Nazca in one of your balloons?"

"Well, I know damned well she didn't arrive in one of your hydrofoils."

102

That broke up breakfast and we walked down to the dock past a dozen grazing llamas. We boarded the Inca Arrow, Darius took the controls and we roared away from the Bolivian coast out upon the tideless waters.

The light is simply fantastic on the Bolivian *altiplano*. It's hard to believe one's light meter——mine registered more brilliance than its solenoid cell could handle. As we raced above the water, we passed several fishermen far from shore in their reed boats. Scores of wild ducks scooted across our bow. I tried to capture the brilliance with my camera but finally gave up and simply drank in the striking scenes that raced by.

Within half an hour we reached the small, rocky Island of the Sun, where a band of Indians stood on the end of the dock to meet us. In the center of the group was a very short, sturdy, impressive old man. I guessed he was the boat builder and I was right.

When we were ashore Darius translated my Spanish to the Quechua-speaking Indians. They had just received news of our project and told us we were lucky, for they had cut reed two weeks earlier and they still had enough of the drying reed to make our "flying boat."

We walked to a large adobe building where most of the village men were gathered and the old man and I talked of the boat he would build. I had brought the two 30-foot lengths of manila rope that the engineers wanted woven into the boat. I showed the old man a drawing that illustrated our idea.

He responded by drawing a very clear cut-away diagram of the reed craft's tubular construction. The old man drew a line through the two widest reed tubes to indicate where they would place our rope. We next agreed the boat would carry two men seated opposite

103

each other. There seemed to be a clear understanding between us and we shook hands.

"It should take him three days," Darius translated. "He asks if you will come back then."

"I'd like to see how he builds it."

After a lengthy discussion Darius said that the old man would show me when I returned in three days When we left the small village, our hydrofoil slid out through the shallow waters, which were thick with totora.

"I'm amazed he can build it so fast," I said.

"He could build your gondola in a day," Darius answered.

"Why three days, then?"

"I think it's to figure out the price. He said they've never sold one before."

I was delighted with the three-day building period, for it gave me an unexpected chance to explore Tiahuanaco and to meet Carlos Ponce Sangines.

I spent the next two days prowling around Tiahuanaco and studying its impressive evidence that ancient man not only had the idea of flight, but certainly the spirit. Tiahuanaco's major site is Kalasasaya, a large sanctuary of massive, superbly dressed volcanic stones built for sun worship. In the ancient temple's northwestern corner stands the renowned Gateway of the Sun (Puerta del Sol), a solid 10-ton block of andesite covered with rows of sharply engraved "condor men."

Row upon row of these "flying men of Tiahuanaco" wear masks of condors and have wings strapped to their arms. They are all racing toward a large god carved above them. The crowning central god may represent the sun or Venus, or, if the giant monolith is a calendar, the highest figure may represent September, the planting month in the Andean world.

To me the ancient men seemed to be straining to

take flight toward their god. They seemed like a flock of modern-day California hang-gliding enthusiasts rushing forward to give their Rogallo wings lift. I made a note to check if there was any modern-day gliding or soaring in Bolivia and later found that La Paz is a center for that exciting sport today. The thermals there are some of the world's best for gliding.

On my second day in Tiahuanaco I roamed the neighboring ruins of Puma Punku, where enormous 100-ton blocks of red sandstone were strewn across the plain by some unknown cataclysmic disaster long, long ago.

In the late afternoon I watched the archeological teams excavating and kept saying no to small boys who would suddenly appear beside me offering a tiny carving or pottery shard for sale. I watched the sun set upon the ancient lake and the moon glisten on the snow-capped high Andes.

The excavating crew started a fire and I joined them as a dark night came on fast. It was cold and the hot *chuño* they cooked went down well with the bottle of Chilean wine I had brought along for such an emergency. Around the glowing campfire I remembered how night was the time for thinking for early man. We sat there talking of Tiahuanaco's tri-millennial past as I watched the smoke curl upward toward the stars.

On my last morning in La Paz, Darius arranged a meeting with the local press and Carlos Ponce Sangines, director of Bolivia's National Archeological Institute. I'd read his authoritative works on Tiahuanaco and wanted his opinion on our project. I have always thought Tiahuanaco had been a central influence in much of the Nazcas' culture.

We met and talked for over an hour, and when I'd finished explaining our objectives at Nazca, Carlos was enthusiastic.

105

"The new experimental Nazca project is very interesting and has a scientific base," he later told the press. "The principle of smoke as the energy for flights above Nazca by no means seems unlikely."

After lunch Darius and I set out for Lake Titicaca. The Indians had sent word that they would deliver the gondola to Huatajata by mid-afternoon. The old man had decided on the price—the equivalent of forty-three U.S. dollars. I was anxious to see his work.

As we drove to the lake we passed through Laja, the lone village on the long straight road across the *altiplano*. A fiesta was in full swing and a band of costumed devil dancers had taken over the main street. Before they would let us pass we had to get out, have a drink with them and chew handfuls of absolutely the largest popcorn I have ever seen. One kernel was a mouthful. A huge costumed white bear with a panting red tongue and a drunk inside was terrorizing the village children. It was with considerable effort that we extracted ourselves from the hilarity.

The moment we pulled into Huatajata I saw a knot of curious Indians surrounding the flying gondola. When we pulled up beside them, I saw that the old man had created a work of art. The reeds were shiny and tightly woven and the gondola's shape was graceful. The builder was beaming.

The old boat builder spent nearly an hour telling me of the gondola's construction and how to care for it. The craft now weighed 132 pounds and was guaranteed to lose several pounds as the reed continued to dry. It was obvious that the old man had created his masterpiece.

The old Indian explained that the normal reed boats he makes are bound by grass twine every five or six inches; but because this one would fly, it had been securely bound every two inches. Moreover, he had ingeniously braced the bottom with light slats of hardwood and thoughtfully woven extra reed into the ends to cushion the vertical impact of landing. I was astonished at his understanding. There was, however, a problem.

When we checked the balance I discovered the error, and it had been mine. I'd told the old man two of us would ride face to face inside the craft. What I had neglected to say was that the two men were both over six feet tall. Our builder was just over four feet and he had built it with himself in mind.

When Darius and I sat inside the gondola, there was simply no room for our legs. If we were to fly, we would have to straddle the reed boat.

"Do you want to spend another forty-three dollars?" Darius asked, laughing.

"No, it's acceptable. It's beautifully made and beautifully balanced, and I don't think it's too heavy. If he would have made it any larger, we would have a weight problem. We'll fly with our legs astride."

Next, the old man proudly showed me the tools he had used to build the gondola—a smooth flat rock and a natural wood hook. I asked him to demonstrate how he had worked with them. With some extra reed he rolled the totora into a long tube, then pounded with the rock as he hooked it tightly with braided grass. He worked fast and surely, and when he finished the demonstration he gave me the tools.

"He wants you to have them," Darius translated, "in case you need to make repairs."

I never knew if the old man was having fun with me or if he was serious. He seemed delighted with the money I paid him and wished me every success in the coming flight. I was again completely astonished that he took the whole idea of flying in a reed boat so nonchalantly. If the ancient Nazca had come here to build their gondolas, they would have certainly been in the right place.

We strapped the 8-foot-long gondola atop our station wagon, secured the inlaid lines and drove back toward La Paz. We arrived at the El Alto airport an hour before the nightly LAB Boeing-727 to Lima. The gondola just barely squeezed inside the cargo hatch.

"The Incas didn't send their gondolas to Nazca in a jet belly," Darious chided. "They would have had to round up a llama train."

"How long from here to there by llama?"

"The last man we sent overland took a year and a half."

"What happened?"

"It wasn't the Andes," he explained. "He met a witch along the way."

8

A Controlled Accident

THE NIGHT FLIGHT ACROSS THE ANDES WAS UN-usually smooth, and as we approached the Pacific the lights of Lima were sparkling below in the moonlight. There was no coastal fog and I could clearly see white-caps as they rolled in toward the port of Callao.

Mike was waiting on the airport apron to help clear the gondola through customs. We finally declared it an "aircraft part" and that seemed to satisfy the horde of officials who rubber-stamped our papers. We loaded the reed boat on a stake truck and drove it downtown to store it in the basement of Mike's office building. The Indians had advised that the gondola be kept in a damp storage place and that the braided grass be moistened once a week with a wet cloth to prevent dry-ing and cracking.

When we'd safely stored the gondola, we walked over to the Bolívar and over dinner brought each other up to date on Project Nazca.

Mike reported that the Peruvian Air Force had given us complete weather information on the Nazca valley, which showed November through January as ideal months for our flight. The weather report read like a ballonist's dream—cold nights, pleasant, still mornings, warm afternoons with surface winds. Throughout the year the hours before and after dawn were almost always calm. November, December and January were reportedly the months without storms.

"There is some change of season in early November

111

that causes slight morning winds from the mountains," Mike added, "but by mid-November Nazca should be quiet. The only hazards are *torremolinos*—windmills. They're a desert version of the waterspouts you have off the Florida coast."

"You mean dust devils?" I asked.

"Yes. They reportedly are very numerous but not considered dangerous. I don't think they'll be a problem, for they don't begin until midday, when the desert heats up. In the afternoon, however, they would be very hazardous to a balloon."

"Any other warnings?"

"No. And you'll be pleased that they finished their report by saying the Nazca valley is ideal for lighter-than-air flight. I suggest you plan to fly the last week of November."

I agreed and we set up a schedule for the coming months. I was glad to have a launch date to work toward. Eight months would give us plenty of time to assemble a good crew and complete Condor I's construction.

Flying back to Miami on the midnight jet, I made a list of what the expedition still needed. There were two outstanding items. First, we had to assemble the best possible ground and inflation team. Second, Bill and I had to learn how to fly Condor I. As there are no schools teaching smoke-ballooning, it looked like we'd return to early aviation's fly-by-the-seat-of-your-pants method.

The next morning in Miami I learned Bill had made a similar list and had just convinced the Explorers Society to buy a brand-new Raven balloon—the 77,000-cubic-foot Model S-55A, already dubbed the "Explorer."

"It's nearly the same cubic size as Condor I," Bill explained excitedly, "and wait until you see her. She's eight stories high—one third larger than The Great Gatsby—and we'll be able to practice flying her with

112

the same gross load we'll carry at Nazca. I guarantee you that by the time Condor I is built, we'll know how to fly her."

Later that day I bought a brand-new crash helmet. Despite Bill being a licensed commercial balloon instructor, some sixth sense told me there would be more problems ahead than we could envision at this stage. Unfortunately, particularly for Bill, that was sadly true.

The next two months, however, were genuinely exciting. We raced through weekdays waiting for weekends, when we'd take the Explorer south of Miami to the farming areas to practice landing our mock smoke balloon with sacks of sand.

The early morning flying weather was almost always excellent. Dawn was calm and the sky was clear. If it weren't for the power lines of Miami, the Everglade swamps and the Atlantic Ocean, south Florida would be a balloonist's paradise. Several times we had to put down before floating into urban Miami, and two or three times we nearly slipped into the Everglades, where recovery would have been very difficult. Only once were we carried by a sudden west wind almost to the ocean.

We spent the weeknights compiling flight data tables for the upcoming week and studying the results of the past weekend. A typical simulated Nazca training flight profile with a free lift of 450 pounds was:

Time (sec.)	Altitude (ft.)	Velocity (f.p.m.)	Remarks
0	0	0	—
10	75	500	—
30	200	500	—
60	300	0	—
75	380	0	—
105	300	−500	—
120	200	−650	Hit Burner

113

We continued several descent tests utilizing ballast instead of "hitting the burner" to arrest our fall. Gradually we learned that the sudden dumping of 100 pounds of ballast as the Explorer was falling at 500 feet per minute would decay our descent velocity to a comfortable 25 feet per minute. We continued running these trajectory flights until we could play out the ballast in 25-pound bags of sand. Our descent trajectory was becoming smooth and controlled. Based on our early training flights, it looked as if the safest flight plan for two men in a super-heated smoke balloon the size of Condor I was to aim for an altitude under 1,000 feet with a flight duration of approximately five minutes.

After a few weekends we felt we were accomplished "smoke balloonists"—at least we knew how to super-heat the Explorer and maintain a controlled descent. Since Condor I would have no maneuvering vent or rip panel, we would be entirely dependent on ballast. The learning process had not been without what the ballooning fraternity calls our share of "high-impact landings."

Once we flew when there was a steady eight-mile-an-hour wind blowing on takeoff. We climbed to 2,000 feet before we realized the wind had suddenly increased considerably. In a balloon one is with the wind—flying freely along with it. It is one of the purest sensations of flight man can possibly know. It can, however, become hazardous when a sudden south Florida squall comes ripping in off Biscayne Bay. We quickly realized our ground speed must be well over thirty miles per hour, for our chase cars below were having difficulty keeping up with us.

We were literally streaking toward downtown Miami when we realized it was either put down in the final tomato field ahead or risk striking a power line in town or a dunking in Biscayne Bay.

We came down fast and hard, and when the wicker hit we bounced a good 30 feet in the air. Bill ripped the top panel out of the Explorer, and the basket and envelope came crashing down together. We were both shaken and bruised. The wind dragged us another 500 feet before the gondola and envelope were caught up in a line of wind-breaking pines. But our worst crash still lay ahead.,

By early July, Bill and I were confident we could control the flight of Condor I. Raven reported that the nearly completed envelope would be ready to air-freight to Peru by mid-September. We began selecting potential crew members from within the Explorers Society and continued looking for someone who knew how to inflate a smoke balloon.

Later that week an invitation came for the Explorers to participate in the annual Seven-Up balloon meet in Columbus, Ohio, on August 25. The annual event offers keen competition for seven of the country's leading hot-air balloons. Bill accepted with the idea that the race would be a good flying warm-up for Nazca.

The Ohio meet also proved to be a good logistical preview of what would be involved in shipping the Nazca balloon. By the time we had crated the envelope and gondola, plus assorted inflation fans, radios, instruments and fuel tanks, the total weight was well over 1,000 pounds. Additionally, we had to recruit a five-man ground crew and hire trucks at the other end. On August 23 we were all aboard a northbound jet for Columbus, with the balloon on a cargo jet just behind.

That afternoon we trucked our equipment to the launch site and went over rules of the upcoming "hare and hound" competition. The next morning at eight a lead "hare" balloon would take off from the Ohio State Fair Grounds. After a five-minute interval, the seven competing "hound" balloons would give chase. The balloon landing closest to the "hare" would win.

115

Modern-day ballooning is a big happy family. At that night's pre-race banquet, the seven competing crews all toasted each other and veteran balloonist Kingswood Sprott topped them all with the traditional salute to Trottie True, "the first woman to be seduced when carried aloft beneath a balloon's soft gutta-percha." Cheers!

Despite the festivities, all pilots and crews were up at six-thirty beginning inflation procedures. A fairly brisk wind came up at seven and the race seemed in jeopardy. At eight the wind was gusting just over ten miles per hour and over a dozen men were struggling to hold the inflated "hare" to the ground. At eight-ten there was a lull and the lead balloon flew quickly away.

Bill and I had drawn the number three takeoff slot, and as we were inflating, the first two balloons flew quickly away. When we were given the signal to lift off, the wind was rising again. We just got off ahead of a nasty gust that caught us about 25 feet above the fair grounds and quickly carried us toward a large ferris wheel that we luckily cleared by a few feet. It was a bad start.

We climbed to 1,800 feet and looked back to watch the last three balloons rise after us. Only two were launched as the wind came up again and forced immediate deflation of the last balloon. The Seven-Up race was on with only six up.

The wind carried us swiftly across Columbus and out into the countryside. We had radio and field glasses on board; both were necessary to keep us aware of the "hare's" position. Increasing winds were rapidly scattering the six balloons as we each searched the varying wind directions at various altitudes.

We flew for nearly an hour before our radio announced the "hare" had landed. We had lost sight of her after half an hour and were trying to keep

King Sprott's Number Two green-and-gold balloon in sight. He had drifted about three miles northeast of us and had flown most of the way at about 1,000 feet. We guessed he had his sights on the Number One balloon.

Bill estimated we were traveling over fifty miles per hour at nearly every altitude we tried. Aside from the wind, it was a glorious day to be racing above the Indian-summer countryside. As we skimmed the fields, children would run and wave, dogs would bark, cars would stop on the narrow farm roads and the drivers would climb out and stare up at us.

"Which way to Toledo?" we would yell, and the startled souls below would point the way.

The race remained very lighthearted until we drifted toward a large lake. We watched King glide across its northern bank as we were heading along the opposite shore. We were in the grip of the wind and, of course, completely unable to steer. We watched King descend swiftly and saw his target. There, just below him, lay the deflated "hare." He was spot on the target and we were floating out across Buckeye Lake. We were headed for a good ride or a wet landing.

The wind over the lake was very strong and what had looked like a long crossing took just twelve minutes. In order to hopefully salvage a second or third place, we decided to land at the first possible spot on the shore. We descended to 500 feet and picked an empty pasture just ahead.

Bill adroitly adjusted the maneuvering vent to speed our descent. The variometer registered our drop at 300 feet per minute. It had been my first really rapid descent and it felt—as I had been warned—like we were stationary and the earth was coming up fast.

We hit with a hell of a jolt and instantly bounced very high. Bill yanked the rip panel out, but the wind still carried us toward a line of trees. We bounced

117

again and dragged through tall grass before the gondola slammed into a row of wind-breaking poplars. We were both upside down but inside the wicker basket.

I had braced myself upon impact, but the radio had flown up and cut my lip. Other than that—bruised fingers and sore knees—I would be all right, but Bill was hurt.

He had wrenched his back badly when we hit. He had been concentrating on the rip lines and had only braced himself with one arm. He had slammed against the propane tanks in the bottom of the basket and was in pain.

He lay there for several minutes asking me not to move him. Our radio was out and we had cut a path through the heavy grass like a threshing machine. We were both covered with dirt, dust and freshly mown hay. I was hoping a spotter plane would radio our position to our chase crew. I knew, however, they were several miles away working their way around the lake.

I was greatly relieved in ten minutes when Bill asked me to help him stand. I could tell he was in agony when he finally stood by holding onto the overturned gondola. The balloon lay tangled in the trees beside us.

Bill had first injured his back in Vietnam and had strengthened it through regular exercise. He was no stranger to the excruciating pain of damaged discs. Somehow he seemed to recover and assured me he would be all right and that I should walk to the nearest road to guide in our chase crew.

It took me only fifteen minutes to find a road and then our truck. I luckily discovered a pair of ruts that led to the poplar windbreak where Bill was managing a painful walk beside the balloon.

"I'll make it," he assured me before adding, "but you're going to have to find someone else for Nazca."

The doctor's diagnosis agreed with that prediction. The next afternoon Bill went into traction in a Miami hospital. Six months from the scheduled flight of Condor I, the project was without a chief pilot.

Just after I left the hospital I received a call from Project Engineer TeKrony in South Dakota. He gave me a progress report on Condor I that confirmed Raven was on schedule. The sewing was nearly completed, the rigging was designed and shipment would be on schedule.

I reported Bill's accident and asked if Ken had any idea who might be a good replacement.

"Considering this an experimental flight," he answered, "and if it were me going up in it, I'd get the best balloon pilot in the world."

"Who's that?"

"I don't know but I'd sure find him."

After I'd hung up the receiver, I decided to take Ken's advice literally. Why not find out who is considered the world's best balloon pilot and ask him if he'd like to join the project?

I was seated at my desk and on the shelf beside me were a dozen reference books. I pulled out the 1975 *Guinness Book of World Records* and looked under "Balloon." There was a listing for "Records" on page 327.

When I found the page it read:

Hot-air-balloon altitude record is 45,837 feet, held by Julian Nott, Great Britain, over Bhopal, India, in Daffodil II, a 375,000-cubic-foot Cameron A-375 balloon on January 25, 1974.

And that is how I met Julian.

119

9

The Explorers

EARLY THE NEXT MORNING A PERSISTENT OVER-seas information operator managed to locate a some-what startled Julian Nott at Campden House in Ken-sington. He agreed to meet me the following day in London.

When I boarded the nonstop National Miami-to-London jet, I'm sure the ancient Nazca looking over my shoulder must have envied today's modern com-munication and transportation systems. To fly a primi-tive balloon these days was certainly taking plenty of long-distance telephoning and jet travel.

Julian suggested we meet for dinner at Crockford's, a smart, private club that is one of London's lead-ing restaurant-casinos. I figured it a good omen to meet the Englishman in a gambling house—it looked as though he might be willing to take a chance from time to time.

The moment he walked into Crockford's, I knew he was Julian Nott. He was tall, athletic and the very epitome of an English gentleman. More importantly, he had that undefinable quality that seems to grace those who hold world records. We sat down to an excellent dinner of cold salmon and talked ballooning.

Julian told of the 1974 Indian expedition that re-sulted in his record-setting altitude flight. He was a veteran of several expeditions and knew well the prob-lems and rewards.

"We selected central India for the weather," he related, "and Bhopal for its nearby railway station and airport. What we didn't realize is that during our entire adventure both the Indian airlines and railway systems were constantly on strike."

As he detailed his India experience, I was convinced he was the man for Nazca. All expeditions into remote areas, for one reason or another, always become far more complicated than one can initially imagine. I was glad Julian understood the realities of planning the flight of a primitive airship in a desolate area.

As we talked I learned Julian was thirty-two, a bachelor, an Oxford graduate, a physicist and the head of his own London aeronautical engineering firm. His enthusiasm for ballooning was unabashed and unbridled. As I began explaining Project Nazca, he politely interrupted.

"I've just read the details of your project in the current *Ballooning* magazine," he said, "and if you've flown over to invite me to participate, I would be very pleased."

I was delighted with his directness and quickly explained that we didn't just want his participation, but to fly Condor I we needed the best balloon pilot in the world.

"I accept," Julian answered and that called for a bottle of Crockford's best champagne to toast our upcoming adventure.

The next morning I met Julian at the venerable British Science Museum, where a permanent display illustrates his formidable ballooning achievements. There he explained several technical problems he had overcome in his record-setting India flight and their relationship to Condor I.

Julian was very concerned about the lack of a maneuvering vent, possible solar gain, the rigging and the flammable cotton material. I gave him a file of Raven blueprints and correspondence, and as we taxied to the airport he continued to ask a variety of questions that ranged from Nazca's weather to the porosity of the envelope's fabric.

Julian agreed to begin computing a proposed flight profile and make plans to be in Miami in early November. We would keep in regular contact via Telex.

"In all fairness," Julian added, "before I accept your invitation and a great deal of free travel and hospitality, I must tell you I have mixed feelings. From my experience, I think your balloon might not fly at all. The material is very porous and may not hold the heat. Also, the rigging seems dangerous. So many disasters have occurred in flying, especially in ballooning, because of pilots taking off against their better judgment. I want you to know that I won't attempt to fly a craft I don't consider airworthy. I also don't believe your theory."

"Then why go?" I asked.

"Jim, you don't understand English winters. A man will do almost anything here to escape to the Southern Hemisphere's sun. Let's give your idea a try."

We shook hands and I headed into passport control. As I flew back to Miami against the prevailing winds, the long flight gave me plenty of time to review everything involved with Project Nazca. I was satisfied that the balloon and gondola would be ready, airworthy and on schedule. Mike was totally reliable with ground support in Peru. With Julian's provisional acceptance to fly, the only real remaining question mark was inflation. We had yet to find the right man for the launch.

When I landed in Miami, Bill and Lucia Houchins of the Explorer staff met me as I walked out of customs. I could tell by their beaming faces that they had good news.

125

"We've found your launch-crew chief," Bill began, "he's probably the only man in the world who could handle the job."

Both of them then went on to describe the unique background of William M. "Doc" Crane of Adair, Iowa, whose story began at the turn of the century when smoke-ballooning was a daring highlight of many country fairs and carnivals. Up until the early 1930s, a few smoke balloonists still managed to survive by working the smaller towns. These daring early fliers would inflate their large smoke-filled muslin balloons and quickly rise high enough to somersault out by parachute over the country crowds. But as biplane stuntmen and wing-walkers began barnstorming the country, the old smoke balloonists began to fade away.

One of the last of these interpid flying men was Captain Eddy Allen of Batavia, New York. In 1932 he taught the art of launching fire-powered balloons to a strong fourteen-year-old lad, Bill Crane. The youngster toured county fairs and carnivals during the last years of Captain Eddy's daredevil balloon-parachute act. Captain Allen taught young Crane how to rig and inflate balloons over the flashing smoke fires of gasoline. The youngster also learned techniques of sewing, patching and recovery.

Young Crane spent seven years with Captain Allen, and, unfortunately, the apprenticeship was not without tragedy. In a final season of smoke-ballooning, Captain Eddy's daughter was killed in an accident over Blackstone, Virginia. Doc Crane learned well the perils, as well as the pleasures, of ballooning.

In World War II the still-young Crane became an army expert in barrage balloons, and today "Doc" owns and operates his own sport balloon manufacturing company, Falcon Balloons of Adair, Iowa.

Bill had talked to Doc Crane at length by phone and

the fifty-seven-year-old ballooning veteran was ready and willing to join us in Peru.

"Did you talk about inflation?" I asked.

"Yes, and Doc has already worked up a suggested procedure that involves twin-pole rigging and a channeled smoke pit."

Bill next went on to detail research into the history of smoke-balloon inflation. He had found several French lithographs of the late 1700s that illustrated various techniques of holding balloon envelopes over smoke.

"After all we've studied," Bill continued, "it's surprising ballooning ever survived. I think more early balloons were burned than ever flew. Most of the early prints show the final anguished moment when the unfortunate aeronaut crashes in flames.

"The first smoke balloonists in America drew mainly on the experience of the French," he reported. "By the mid-1800s balloon launching was down to a fine art. Doc Crane may well have been the last man to have learned that art firsthand. I don't think anyone younger, who's alive today, has ever launched a smoke balloon."

"Does Doc Crane see any problems with Condor I?" I asked.

"He's never inflated one that size. He's confident it can be smoked—or cured, as he calls it—enough to give you lift. He sounds like a positive man. Talking to him, I got the impression that, if anyone could launch you, it would be Doc Crane."

The next morning when I called Adair, Iowa, I agreed with Bill. The strong, confident voice on the other end of the line gave me a Nazca shopping list that included over 2,000 feet of half-inch rope plus a pair of straight wooden poles 40 feet high.

"I'll also need a good crew of twelve reliable men

127

and another twenty bodies," he added. "And don't worry, we'll get her up."

Just after I'd finished talking to Doc, the phone rang. It was Ken TeKrony at Raven, advising me that the balloon envelope was ready for shipment and asking if he and Jim Winkler could come along.

"Sure," I said. "We're going to need all the able-bodied engineers we can find at Nazca, and make sure you bring a shovel—I think Doc Crane has a place for all of us digging smoke pits."

It was now less than sixty days from our projected flight. We could easily finish the hand-sewing of the envelope in Lima in a week. The gondola was in Peru. Julian was ready and Doc was set—the major problems seemed solved.

In the next two weeks we selected the remaining crew members from within the Explorers' Society. Rounding out the Nazca team were: a veteran balloonist, John Mickel, as ground-crew chief and back-up pilot; Peace Corpsman Jay Hasheider, the expert in Latin American aboriginal and Indian balloons who was named to head up the base camp team; artist Tommy Thompson, a student of pre-Columbian design, who would paint the Nazca symbols on the envelope, a challenging task; and distaff Explorers Lucia Houchins, Christina Howe and my wife, Lisa, who would handle our portable Telex and air-to-ground communications systems.

Rounding out the launch crew would be Junior Explorers representing the teen-age membership: Mike Trebilcock, Les Blanchard, plus my sons, Henry and Jim. At Nazca, Guillermo Elias had been named project coordinator to contract several men to join the expedition.

The next few weeks raced by smoothly. On November 10 we transferred our base of operations from Miami to Lima, and expedition members began arriving in the Peruvian capital. The 550-pound balloon envelope was too large for a DC-8 belly and had to be palletized and shipped via special LAN-Chile cargo jet. When it arrived intact, we began sewing the final seams and rigging the maze of lines. Land-Rovers and trucks were rented and loaded.

Suddenly it was November 18—the day we had set to leave Lima for the desert. As we trouped out of the hotel, I thought we somewhat resembled a traveling band of bullfighters bound for a *corrida* in the provinces. We had that same bit of circus atmosphere, and an apprehensive excitement began to gnaw in the pit of our stomachs.

10

South to Nazca

WE LEFT AT SIX A.M., WHEN LIMA'S NARROW side streets were deserted and just a few of the city's antique, smoky buses were rambling down the main boulevards. The drive south into the stark coastal desert was a relief from the mad traffic we had battled in the Peruvian capital.

We drove the narrow highway, which curves beside giant mountains of sand and the gray Pacific. The coastal fog was thick as we motored on in the misty gray past scores of huge chicken ranches that lay beside the sea. The hens here are fed fish meal and the eggs they lay taste of the sea. We stopped at the small village of Chincha Alta for a sturdy breakfast of steaming fried *corvina* (a sweet, white-meat fish caught off Puerto San Juan, fifty-five miles away on the Pacific), rice and strong *café* made from a condensed coffee syrup.

After breakfast we continued south along the coast as the sky began to brighten noticeably. We passed wide, immense, empty beaches where endless sets of perfect breakers rushed toward shore. It was a surfer's paradise—without surfers.

Just after the Paracas cut off, we drove inland, where the Pan American Highway turns toward the provincial capital of Ica. Slowly the valley became an oasis, the sky cleared and a bright sun lit the faraway mountains. Suddenly what had just been tones of gray turned to the full range of earth colors under a blue, cloudless sky.

Along the road the vineyards of Peru's wine country stretched to the horizon. Bougainvillaea, lattices of climbing vines, giant sunflowers and painted adobe homes brightened the contours of the countryside. The air was warm, yet the wind that still came from the sea was cool. Our lead truck sped along with our gondola lashed atop the heavy balloon crate. The Land-Rover followed to keep watch upon the lashings. By noon we had reached the cool palm-shaded streets of Ica, and after lunch we headed farther south to Santa Cruz, Rio Grande and Palpa.

Between Santa Cruz and Palpa we crossed a rugged mountain range where narrow tunnels just allowed the gondola to pass. Often we stopped to check the balloon lashing as we climbed steep grades. When the highway, now a very narrow asphalt ribbon, neared the town of Palpa, the topography changed dramatically. We left the purple mountains behind and began climbing toward a burnt umber plain that stretched across the wide horizon. It was the great plain that led to Nazca.

As we drove the final twenty miles, we climbed out upon the vast Nazca *pampas*. The narrow highway cut across a great sun-baked vastness that simmered in the early afternoon heat. Always ahead were slick, shiny mirages, and out across the rock-strewn plains we saw an endless silver illusion.

Julian called me from the Land-Rover on the walkie-talkie when he spotted a whirling "dust devil" sucking up a column of sand and racing crazily across the dusty, rocky plain.

"I don't like the looks of that," his English voice cracked over the speaker. "If the wind is kicking up that much at ground level, I wonder what's happening at 500 or 1,000 feet."

We talked briefly of the one lurking danger that worried us most—the stress factor in a cotton balloon. A tough modern-day sport balloon of nylon or rayon could withstand stress far better than could the cotton fabric that would carry us aloft. An unseen tunnel cloud, whirling unnoticed above the dusty plain, would be a very nasty surprise.

We drove on several miles watching a score of the tunnel clouds race pell-mell across the huge expanse of plains, dipping here and there to suck up columns of dust. We noted the time was three-thirty P.M. At best, the whirling tunnel clouds were only an afternoon phenomenon. It was a new worry we would have to recheck.

Ahead lay another range of low, dark, russet-colored hills that stood between us and Nazca. We drove on toward them, straining to see any trace of the great lines and runways from our truck windows.

But there was no trace, no line, no runway, no giant spider or monkey or spiral that we could see. There was only the seemingly endless plain that stretched dramatically and endlessly away from both sides of the road. In the far distance a low line of purple marked the high mountains that ring Nazca.

Before we had ever driven across the plains, we had often talked derisively of the thoughtless engineers and surveyors who unwittingly had constructed the Pan American Highway straight across this archeological treasure. But now, driving through the heart of the plains, we understood. There was nothing on either side of the road that even hinted at what surrounded us. It was only when we came upon a bright orange sign announcing ZONA ARQUEOLOGIA that we knew we were there. As we drove on, we forgave the road builders; they, as we, could see no trace of the treasures that surrounded us.

We read the billboard that warned we would be arrested and our car impounded if we left the highway and cut tire tracks into the *pampas*. We drove on slowly still looking, still scanning each side of the road for signs of the lines—but there were none. The plains of Nazca are a ground-level disappointment. After ten miles the long, straight road began a gradual descent. The unique, appealing face of Nazca lay ahead. We drove toward the silhouette of the town, which stood in a green valley just beneath a colossal mountain seemingly crowned by sand.

It was mid-afternoon when we arrived. The Pan American Highway ran straight to our hotel, and we pulled into a high-walled parking compound before checking into the state-operated hostelry. I received permission from the manager to spread out Condor I upon the dusty soccer field beside the hotel in order to finish sewing and to begin painting the Nazca designs upon the cloth.

After a luncheon of tender lamb, we began the balloon's first unpacking. We needed ten men to carry the 1,000-pound crate from the truck. We carried the mountain of fabric to the center of the dusty field to unravel its fiber lines and cotton panels.

Project artist Tommy Thompson directed that first roll out. We found the balloon's leather crown and then unraveled toward the tetrahedron's ears. The huge fabric was too large for the soccer field, and with Tommy directing a dozen men we were finally able to uncover a projected design area and begin laying out the first symbol. From the Nazca plains we first selected a condor figure to decorate the balloon. It was the obvious choice, for there are eighteen giant bird-like drawings inscribed on the *pampas*. We decided to reproduce the largest on Condor I, and, like all Nazca ground drawings, it was a single, bold, continuous line.

Next we chose a spiral for the tetrahedron's second triangular panel. There are three major spirals drawn upon the Nazca plains. Two are independent spirals that stand alone, and the third is attached to the needle and ball of yarn. After Ken TeKrony had chosen the spiral sewing technique to construct Condor I, we considered the spiral symbols as ancient blueprints for the construction of a flying fabric.

The balloon's third panel would be the sun god—we had taken a line drawing of the smiling Inca deity from ancient pottery. For colors, Tommy chose vivid blue, earth brown and deep orange from dyes he had found on ancient Nazca textiles.

In the late afternoon, as Lucia Houchins hand-sewed the balloon's final critical seams, Tommy laid out string and stones to measure the curves and angles of his projected drawings. His designs had been scaled from the plains, and he reproduced them with bold, single-stroke, six-inch lines upon the cotton panels.

The sun was low as he painted the final wing of the condor. In the soft Nazca sunset, we watched the balloon slowly begin to change from endless bolts of raw white cotton fabric into the airship we had designed.

I was fascinated to see the symbol give the fabric a new dimension. Tommy and I had often talked of the vitality in Nazca's ancient symbols and how they seemed a strange but powerful blend of primitiveness and sophistication. Now as I watched the condor design take shape, I thought of the broad range of meaning that may be contained in every ancient symbol. In the Sahara the Mahalbi drew sketches of animals in the sand and at dawn sprinkled them with blood. In the southwestern U.S.A., Navajos often drew symbols in the sand and laid their sick over them. The Nazca may have walked the lines of their great bird symbols to capture the power of flight. It is frustrating to recognize a symbol and not know its ancient implications.

My fascination with the symbols was evidently

shared by more than a hundred Nazca children. They ringed the balloon and were all staring with wide brown eyes at the great white tapestry being decorated with their ancient art.

"El globo," they repeated, meaning "the balloon."

It was the first time they, or most of us on the project, had seen the craft we would fly. Even there, flat against the dusty field, with its edges tucked in and its major lines hidden, Condor I was massive. When Tommy finished painting, we posted guards around the edges as it dried. The crowd continued to grow and by nightfall nearly a thousand villagers circled the field, standing there to stare at the strange new Condor of Nazca.

While Tommy had been painting, I paid a late-afternoon visit to the mayor's office. Alcalde Enriqui Ricci Bohorquez was cordial and enthusiastic about our project. I needed to obtain his permission to use a small area on the government-owned plains as our launch site.

I told him we had three requisites for a site. First, we didn't want to endanger or molest any of the lines, ground drawings or runways. Second, we wanted to be near a road or trail that could be used by our trucks. Third, we wanted a safe place to fly—no dangerous landing or takeoff obstacles or hazards.

Both of us then studied a detailed map of the region. The mayor and his coterie of lieutenants agreed that our best potential site would be somewhere upon the plains just past the ancient ruins of Cahuachi.

I was delighed with the choice. Cahuachi was where we had found the textile samples that had been used in building the balloon. I knew the plains just beyond the ancient cemeteries were perfect. It was agreed that we could inspect the Cahuachi area the next morning, and if it was to our liking we would have the mayor's permission. That evening we all gathered in the small hotel dining room for an early dinner. Both Julian and I were anxious to visit our proposed launch site to check the pre-dawn wind and weather. Reveille was set for two A.M. It was the last night we would enjoy even a brief sample of the luxury of sleep.

11

Countdown
on the Desert

I AWOKE WITH THE NIGHTWATCHMAN'S FIRST knock. As I quickly dressed I could hear him walking the quadrangle patio to wake most of the launch crew. By two-fifteen A.M. we were all in the Land-Rover and heading out onto the dark *pampas* under the bright starlit sky.

Within ten minutes we were on the flat tableland. Guillermo Elias, our project director in Nazca, sat beside me as we sped along the Pan American Highway. Guillermo was "Mr. Nazca" as far as we (and most of Nazca's female population) were concerned. He was born and raised in the valley and literally knew everyone. He operates the local flying service, the newest hotel and, as the head of Nazca's Flying Club, he has probably logged more air hours over the plains than anyone alive. He had hired several local men to join our launch team, and they followed behind us in an open pickup truck.

We drove on for thirty minutes in the darkness. Our lights and those of the Land-Rover and truck behind were the only signs of life upon the *pampas*. Now a brilliant crescent moon hung just above the high peaks to the east. All around us the Nazca plain ran to the horizon and the sky, full of stars, came straight down to its very edge. We sped on and entered the archeological zone.

"Take a left on the dirt road ahead," Guillermo ad-

143

vised. "It runs back across the plains at a forty-five degree angle from the Pan American Highway and continues fifteen kilometers to Cahauchi."

We turned off the asphalt road and bumped onto a rocky washboard road that pointed straight ahead across the seemingly endless plain. Moonlight cast soft shadows over the deep potholes that gutted the rutted road. We drove slowly, usually in low, to climb a rut or descend into the rocky remains of an ancient flash flood. We rattled on in the bright light of the moon and stars toward the spot we would inspect as a launch site.

As we moved across the *pampas,* I couldn't help feeling the desolation, the isolation, the immenseness of it all. Here was a vast plain cut only by a tiny trail of a road, broken by no tree, no bush, no sign of man —nothing between us and the far horizon.

Within half an hour we had driven deep out across the ancient drawing board of the Nazca. From the sky we must have looked like a tiny trail of light slowly moving on. After we'd fought the rocky road for half an hour, Guillermo advised us that we were nearing the launch area the mayor had suggested. We slowed even more from that point on as we looked carefully out at the seemingly unchanging, rock-strewn, absolutely flat plain.

"It all looks the same to me," I told Guillermo.

"There are differences," he answered. "For the next few kilometers the rocks are much smaller and there is more loose sand."

"Are we near the archeological zone?" Julian asked.

"No, it's well behind us," the Peruvian answered.

We slowed down and decided to inspect the area. We'd been driving nearly fifty minutes from town and hadn't wanted a launch site more than an hour's drive away.

"What's that ahead?" Julian suddenly asked.

144

Before Guillermo answered, the headlights clearly lit a human skull beside the road. It lay there upon the moonlit sand with its jaw missing and dark shadows where its eyes had once been. It was the one foreign object we had seen upon the plains.

"My God, what an omen!" Julian exclaimed.

"Get used to them," Guillermo advised him. "Cahuachi is a graveyard. You'll find skulls and bones and graves from here on."

We stopped to inspect the unexpected skull.

"Well," Julian reasoned with customary British aplomb, "here we are outside the Archeological Zone, on the only road, and where the rocks are small and the sand is soft. I say this chap was placed here to mark the spot."

We pulled the Land-Rover off the road and found the sandy soil still firm enough for our four-wheel-drive to take us in an arc 200 yards from the road. The rocks were smaller here, and there were spots of firm, adobe-like soil that would suit the fire pit we planned. The horizon ran straight and level in all directions, and there was an unbroken vista to the horizon.

The site looked promising. I was delighted with such a find on the first stop. Even more important, the weather was as promised. There was not a cloud, not a whisper of wind. The calm was unique to Julian.

"There is absolutely no wind," he said, "I mean absolutely *none*. What a perfect place to fly a balloon!"

There was no sound, either, nor any moving object. It was absolute desolation and starkly beautiful. We were alone there in the center of the Nazca plains looking at the distant hills in the dark purple light.

"This is a magical place," Julian remarked, summing up all our feelings.

"The old graveyards are just fifteen minutes from

145

here," Guillermo said. "You can't see from here, but there's a ravine about eight kilometers to the southwest. Down in that cut lies Cahuachi, where there are fresh water and Indians who work a small cotton farm. They could be handy if we need more workers. I think this is your place."

"I'm sold," I said, and Julian agreed.

We decided to stake off an 80-square-meter area 200 meters from the road as our launch area. The city officials had asked us to pace off an area that size and they would officially draw up a permit for us to use the land for the launch. Even in the remote Nazca plains there was the need for rubber stamps and triplicate copies to ensure a one-week lease of 80 square meters.

As we measured the site, the eastern sky was slowly brightening with the first slanting signs of morning light. The darkness around us was deep purple and the Southern Cross was low in the windless sky. We waited and worked there in the cold morning air watching for dawn and measuring wind and temperature every fifteen minutes.

Since our readings had begun at three-fifteen A.M., there had been no wind and the ground temperature had stood near 58 degrees. At four-thirty the sky was brightening considerably over the far eastern mountains and we felt a slight rustle of wind that seemed to come from the southeast. It was just a faint breeze, but we could feel it on our faces as we looked toward the approaching sunrise.

The gentle wind was not enough to disturb the falling sand we trickled out of our hands, but by four-fifteen there were occasional gusts that measured four miles per hour on our wind gauge. It was not a steady wind, but rather an occasional rush of slow, cool air that seemed to roll across the *pampas*.

"Those gusts will bear watching," Julian said as a

146

test handful of sand blew away from him toward the north. It was slight, that wind—but it was there.

By five the sky was very light and we began to photograph the stark site we had chosen in the moonlight. It seemed to measure up as well in the growing light as it had in the darkness. Now the dark rocks and black sands turned deep earth colors. An artist would need tubes of burnt umber, dark orange and brown to paint the Nazca *pampas* at dawn. The sky remained totally cloudless and clear as it quickly turned from pale to aquamarine in the early light.

We walked over the ground we had chosen in the darkness. The pits and trench would be dug in a dark brown area of finely packed, dried, mud-like soil. Condor I could be spread out upon a sandy area nearby, from which we'd have to clear away small, sharp rocks. The access from the road proved solid enough to support our truck and, most importantly, we couldn't see any traces of ancient ground drawings or lines in the area.

At five-eighteen the sun burst from behind a mountain on the horizon. Suddenly the colors we had remarked on earlier were now even richer and the scene far more spectacular. The smallest rocks glistened, the sand reflected the sunshine and the mountains grew into vivid shadows. Nazca became magnificent before the rising sun.

As we watched the dawn, I understood how the ancient men who had stood here before us would have worshipped the sun. Its rise was dramatic and alive. It brought life to the plains—it was the ultimate.

"How do you like what you picked in the darkness?" Guillermo asked.

"It's perfect," I said. "We'll spend most of our time here at night, so maybe it's just as well that's when we found the place."

147

"There's a good sign," Julian interrupted, pointing upward.

There, 300 feet above, riding an early morning thermal, was a soaring condor. The magnificent bird was effortlessly riding an updraft and gliding above us without notice.

"That does it for me," Julian said. "That bird balances out any bad omen that skull might hold. If this spot is good enough for a condor, it's good enough for me."

We all shook hands and I asked Guillermo to have the mayor draw up the lease. As we boarded the trucks for the long drive back to town, the condor was still high above us. He was the last we were ever to see upon the plains.

When we reached Nazca, Tommy was painting the spiral symbol on the balloon. We could hardly see him or the fabric because word had traveled through town that the *globo* would be spread out agan for painting. Already nearly a thousand townsfolk circled the balloon.

After a quick breakfast we decided to start hunting for launch supplies. Doc Crane had prepared a list of materials we needed to find in Nazca, and we were determined to find them all locally—as the ancients had. We took Doc's list and began with the first item, firewood.

Ideally, we wanted a very dry wood that would produce an intense heat without creating sparks. The danger of a fiery spark was one of our major worries. At the final stages of inflation, a spark fire in the crown of Condor I would be disastrous.

Our list also called for two large poles for launch support, 1,300 feet of half-inch rope, 700 feet of quarter-inch rope, thirty wooden stakes, plus crew supplies. In addition, Guillermo would have to recruit at least half a dozen strong local workers to complement our own team.

We decided that the wood and poles were the most critical items on the list, and with Guillermo's aid we went first to the local firewood dealer. Our good luck continued, for when we found the wood depository, they had just what Doc had ordered—a very dry supply of local hardwood. The wood had been cut two years earlier and had been stacked ever since outside in the sun—and in all that time it had never once rained.

We spent the next two hours asking villagers where we could find a pair of 40-foot poles and were discouraged until we learned that a large outlying *hacienda* had just cut down some old, tall Eucalyptus trees. When we arrived at the colonial ranch, we found a pair of very straight, very heavy 40-foot trunks that would serve us well.

The heat of the Nazca day was coming up fast, and by eleven A.M. I'd made arrangements for the town's largest truck to haul the firewood and poles out to the site in the late afternoon. At eleven-thirty we washed the dryness of the desert down with a cool liter of beer, and we all went to bed for the midday *siesta* that was to become our routine—and our only real sleep—in the days to come.

At four we assembled a six-man work crew that Guillermo had contracted and hauled the firewood, poles and ourselves out to the launch site. Now Doc Crane was in charge and he proved the right man for what lay ahead.

We had planned to draw on Doc's old-time smoke balloon techniques and blend them with what we had learned of the ancient use of fire. The burn pits within the Nazca lines had convinced us that the ancient flying men had built large fires upon the plains. The charred rocks that still lie there are convincing evidence of great ceremonial blazes that long ago lit the *pampas*. We planned to recreate one of those fires.

Our first task was to dig a pit and trench. As Doc paced off the area to excavate, the large truck we'd rented pulled up beside the proposed pit and it took ten of us to unload the heavy 40-foot poles and lay them out upon the rocky *pampas*.

Next Doc staked the area to be excavated. He marked off a 10-by-10-foot square, and a three-man shovel team began to dig. Doc wanted the main fire pit to be four feet deep. As we dug into the rocky ground, we began to appreciate what it had been like for the ancients to dig their 20-mile-long trenches with stone implements. It took three busy men with large, sharp shovels over half an hour to build our small fire pit.

As the pit was being dug, Julian and Doc made their final decisions on wind direction. Doc's idea was to orient the fire pit and trench to any prevailing pre-dawn wind to creat a natural flue. Bush pilot Joe Pauley had said that the slight prevailing winds of early morning would come from the south, and he was certain any gusts would also come from that direction. We had also learned that by mid-morning the winds often shifted slightly to the south-southeast and by noon strong winds came from the west.

Next Doc laid out a 25-foot trench that would lead from the fire to what he called the smoking pit. The trench would be oriented to the wind and begin at the fire pit's base and evenly incline up toward the shallower smoke pit. It was over the smoke pit that we would suspend the mouth of the balloon to capture the energy from the fire. To prevent any caving in, we planned to line the trench with fired adobe bricks.

When the sweating crew finished the fire and smoking pits, they began the narrow tunnel. Doc had them begin midway between the two pits. They dug a two-foot-square hole three feet deep. From both ends of this hole, two-man teams began carving a slanting trench in both directions.

By the time we had completed our digging, the Nazca sky was streaked with a bright orange and red glow that resembled an Arizona sunset. Next the Junior Explorers lined the pits with fired adobe and covered the narrow smoke trench with green bamboo to complete the tunnel between the fire and the balloon.

Doc surveyed the trench as it was being covered. "No spark should be able to travel those twenty-five feet and still have enough left to burn our fabric," he said.

As night moved onto the plains, the glow of the dying sunset softened the *pampas* and the Nazca sky paled in those moments before the first stars began to appear. With the sun gone, the air became cool and so refreshing that we decided to continue working.

Our next move was to erect support stakes that would frame the giant balloon during inflation. Doc marked spots for two more holes forty feet to the right and left of the smoke pit's center. These were to be one-foot-deep circles that would hold the base of the tall Eucalyptus trunks. We quickly dug them out and rolled the base of the logs beside each.

The twin poles would be held in place with three long ropes tied to stakes eighty feet away. The ropes would both anchor and support the huge poles. When one line was cut, the pole would instantly fall back toward the cut line's stake. It was a simple, yet ingenious, support technique.

"Would the ancient men here ever have devised a breakaway rig like this?" I asked Doc as he was marking off measurements.

"They would have come up with something like it,"

he answered assuredly. "I know Eddy Allen devised this technique after experimenting with a variety of ways to hold a balloon's mouth over fire."

As we drove in the stakes, I thought of Nazca's wide trapezoids and the large fire pits over which we had flown and walked. They were certainly as wide as our launch area, which now measured 240 feet across.

When the final stake had been driven in, Doc began rigging 80-foot guy ropes from the tops of the poles to each stake. When the lines had been measured, cut and tied, we erected the first pole. It took six of us to center the heavy Eucalyptus trunks in their shallow base trenches. When each pole was straight to Doc's eye, a man at each stake tied his line taut.

Both poles went up surprisingly quickly. I thought their weight would make them difficult to align, but they now stood firmly erect in their base holes, each secured tightly by three staked ropes. By eight o'clock the fire pit, smoke hole and trench were dug, and our launch site was ready for the balloon.

We all climbed into the now-empty trucks and drove back across the Nazca plains toward town. That afternoon and evening we had not seen anyone or anything on the *pampas*. No condor had flown over, no desert animal, no sound, no life—nothing but the stark plain had surrounded us. We had been completely alone on the vast, empty tableland. Only the strong, gusting afternoon wind and countless swirling funnel clouds had distracted us from our work.

At the hotel we dined on a hot noodle soup laced with fiery orange peppers. The main course was *corvina*. We all tumbled into bed before nine and left our usual call for two A.M.

12
Tunnel of Smoke

THE DAY BEGAN AS USUAL IN THE MIDDLE OF the night. By two-fifteen A.M. our headlights were piercing the darkness of the plains, and by three we had reached our launch site. As we approached I saw our two giant poles rising above the flat, monotonous moonlit plains. We turned right at the skull and Julian quickly set up our portable weather station.

At three A.M. there was no wind—not a quiver on the anemometer. The temperature was 57 degrees and the bright, star-filled sky was cloudless.

"Another perfect morning to balloon," Julian commented as he wrote in the weather log. "I've never seen such stillness like this last three consecutive days anywhere—including the Sahara and India."

By four-forty-five the sky was bright and we knew from past mornings that the sun would break over the mountaintops at about five-fifteen. Our first few mornings on the Nazca plains were absolutely magnificent. As we watched the day be born, we felt the enormity of the desert sun. It is a spectacular sight to watch the formation of a day in Nazca's immense natural theater. When those first warm, beautiful rays of light initially spilled over the peak, it was enough to make sun worshippers of us all.

On this morning Jay Hasheider was set to launch his first test balloon. Young Jay, a dedicated Peace Corps volunteer stationed in El Salvador, had been given a short leave to join Project Nazca. His balloon credentials were impressive, and he'd made an extensive study of the surviving ceremonial smoke balloons still used by Central and South American Indians today.

Jay had seen scores of smoke balloons launched by Indian tribes in El Salvador, Guatemala and Peru. The practice of launching smoke balloons on special occasions is traditional throughout Latin America, and has been for centuries. For as long as tribes can remember, model balloons have been launched in the Andes. In Guatemala ceremonial balloons are often made from dried animal intestines that are pierced and patched together and fired aloft filled with smoke and prayers to the gods.

In El Salvador high-flying globes are now made of light tissue paper. In the mountains of Peru the natives use thin paper greased with animal fat. Everywhere these ritual balloons are launched by holding them over the smoke of an open fire or a burning wad of kerosene-soaked cotton.

We had decided to test Nazca's wind current and direction at various altitudes with these Indian balloons. Jay constructed a simple six-foot balloon from tissue paper patterned after those the Indians of rural Peru use today.

To inflate the test balloon, Jay had soaked a small cotton wad in gasoline and then strung it just inside the balloon's mouth. When he lit the soaked cotton it burst into flames and the sudden rush of hot air and smoke quickly filled the paper globe. Lisa held the top and sides, and when it was fully expanded, she let it free. We watched the paper globe rise quickly away from her hands and fly straight up into the cloudless sky.

The test balloon climbed quickly, dead straight above us, to 500 feet. It continued on its timed release to 1,000 feet without signaling a trace of wind. At about 1,500 feet a soft wind began pushing it northwest. As it climbed past 2,000 feet, the wind directions changed twice—the air at higher altitudes above us was curiously variable. We watched the balloon—now a tiny yellow spot against the early morning sky—continue to rise for nearly six minutes. Then, perhaps at just over 4,000 feet, it began a slow descent to the rocky *pampas* floor.

We followed the trial balloon on foot, and as it began falling Jay ran to catch it. The smoldering wick would ignite the flimsy paper if it would crash. If one can catch the falling models, they may be saved and flown again. From over a mile away we watched Jay sprint the final few yards to catch his balloon. He snared it just before it touched the rocky plains.

It was a good omen—our first inflation, flight and recovery had been a success. Also, the wind was nonexistent from ground level up to almost 1,500 feet. It was an encouraging test and we felt much as Bartolomeu Gusmão might have when his first paper model—powered by charcoal instead of a flaming cotton ball—lifted off in the court of Lisbon centuries ago.

When Jay returned to the pit area with the small, deflated balloon, we all congratulated him on the first flight over the Nazca plains in the last one thousand years. Julian packed up his weather station and we all piled into the trucks and Land-Rovers for the long drive back to town and a welcome breakfast.

When we finished the thick bacon, eggs and hot coffee, Doc announced what was to become our schedule for the days to come. He suggested sleep until mid-afternoon, followed by lunch, and then, in the cooler, late afternoon hours, work at the site.

Dinner was set for eight, followed by two or three hours of sleep until midnight, when everyone would depart for the launch site. Doc also assigned launch responsibilities—team members were named for the fire pit, major support lines, fire control and holding. That afternoon I had reserved one of Joe Pauley's light aircraft to give everyone on the launch team the opportunity to fly over the Nazca lines.

While our crew went sightseeing, Julian and I returned to the site with a checklist of everything needed to fly Condor I. The list was long and included such diverse items as needle and thread to patch burn holes, heavy burlap bags for ballast and buckets of sand to be used as fire extinguishers.

As we drove out upon the plains and through the archeological zone, we again vainly searched for ground-level traces of the lines and markings that had drawn us to Nazca in the first place. But it is frustratingly unrewarding to search the flat, rocky *pampas* on the ground for clues to what is drawn there. Today, however, as we drove out toward the launch site, we saw Joe's Cessna-172 circling in the distance.

"They're probably over the monkey," Julian said pointing.

"It looks like Joe found it today," I answered, remembering bush pilot Pauley's continuing problem in finding the famous drawing. In his hundreds of flights over the Nazca lines, Joe would first begin his tour with a view of the long runways, then the lines, and he would end with a low-level look at the giant ground drawings. Often after flying through the maze of lines, one can easily misjudge the monkey's position.

"Me and that monkey keep going 'round and 'round," Joe had said late one afternoon as we had skimmed low over the plains for a final look at the animal figure. Nazca is such a maze from above that it is bewildering even to the most experienced of pilots.

It was late afternoon now, and as the Cessna made

158

lazy circles to the west I knew how amazed our launch crew would be as they stared down at the markings. I now think late afternoon is the best time to see and photograph the Nazca markings; for the light of the setting sun slants across the engraved lines and casts clear shadows that accentuate their shapes from above.

As we drove on, the Cessna disappeared. By the time we'd reached the site, Joe was overhead again with more of our crew seeing Nazca—*really* seeing Nazca—for the first time.

We ran over the launch checklist: rope, poles, firewood, pits, tunnel, adobe, charcoal, repair materials and tools. Everything was ready for the first fire in the early morning hours tomorrow. Just before leaving, the Cessna buzzed us as three more of our astonished crew members flew back toward town fueled with new enthusiasm and new speculation on what they had seen.

That evening the dinner table was a hotbed of ideas, theories and admiration concerning the lines and the ancients who created them. The highlights of the afternoon flights had been Joe's low-level approach near a figure we had not seen before—a large drawing of a huge ancient Nazca etched into a rock face. The friendly ancient character was waving, his right hand extended over his head, obviously greeting those passing in the sky. The effect was electrifying to our ground crew.

"When I saw the lines and the figures that we had driven past without being able to see, I couldn't believe it," Jay remarked, "and then when I saw this friendly little man there waving at me, I was dumbfounded. All of us on our flight waved back."

That brought a big laugh and we all continued discussing how well the lines were camouflaged to ground observers.

"Had they been visible," Guillermo said, "they would have been mutilated long ago. The lines have been popular during the last five years, and in that time the ones nearest the highway have nearly been obliterated by tourists vainly driving out on the pampas hoping to see something. That's why all of us in Nazca are so thankful for the program to protect Nazca that the International Explorers have started. Your $1,000 donation has really started things moving."

By nine the conversation began to give way to yawns, and we retired to try and sleep the three remaining hours before midnight; but most everyone lay awake and thought over their afternoon flight above the lines. There are few symbols in our world that ancient man has left us that are as dramatic, as intriguing, as mysterious and as unforgettable as are those at Nazca.

Wednesday began with a midnight knock on the door by the hotel's old watchman, who by now was convinced we were all totally mad. No one had ever come to Nazca and gone out to the plains every night at midnight or two A.M. The large gates of the hotel's parking compound swung open and by twelve-thirty we were all on the moonlit rocky road leading to the launch site. Our objective tonight was to experiment with the fire that would smoke the porous fabric of Condor I.

The heavy, dry hardwood logs we'd found in the cutter's yard were stacked beside the fire pit. Guillermo assured me no drier wood existed in the valley. With a machete we shaved and splintered a sizeable pile of shavings and sticks to begin the fire. Instantly the kindling blazed and within ten minutes we were laying large logs atop a good bed of glowing coals. The bright fire spread a warm glow across the launch site. The poles and ropes stood out in the soft orange firelight. The wood burned well, no crackling, no sparks— an intense, scorching heat rose from the deep pit.

160

A slight ruffling breeze came up at two-thirty and for a moment visibly fanned the fire despite its being deep in the pit. Even before the wind started, the smoke seemed to be drawn naturally through the narrow tunnel toward the open smoke pit. Doc's idea was working well. Nothing but hot, blue smoke—no sparks—curled skyward. As we stood there watching the thick smoke billow upward, our clothes became saturated with its scent. From then on the smell and taste of smoke would stay with us all.

Doc decided to fuel the fire to its limit. With the longer logs we pushed several coals far into the tunnel mouth and then slid new logs in on top of them. This seemed to increase the draft, and the fire became white-hot and dense smoke billowed from the trench. The wood fire was producing far more heat than we had anticipated.

"That's absolutely the driest wood I've ever seen!" Doc yelled above the fire's roar. "That'll out-produce any propane you modern balloonists could find."

All of us stood ringing the fire and John and Henry, who had the responsibility for stoking, had to shield their faces every time they neared the flames to add wood or attempt to push coals farther up into the tunnel.

None of us had realized how hot the fire had become. Soon the sandy edges of the tunnel and the fired adobe brick were turning crisp black. We had naïvely placed green bamboo logs across the smoke tunnel and now watched them smolder and catch fire. Soon the bamboo burned or fell into the tunnel and smoke was everywhere. We stopped fueling the flames and for an hour watched the fire die. When it had cooled we cleared the tunnel to remove what was left of the caved-in bamboo. Despite the fact we had seen no sparks, Doc decided the tunnel was vital to protect the

161

balloon from fire, and we decided to rebuild it without the bamboo.

"The first people who flew here could have just held their textile bag over an open fire to catch the smoke," Doc said, "but you know damned well they probably burned up a few. That wood gets so hot that I want space between it and the mouth of Condor I."

While the crew dug out the hot coals and cleared the tunnel, we decided to deepen the entire fire pit area. We would then form a corbel arch of fired abode over the tunnel. All of us worked until dawn clearing and deepening the pits and trenches. The Junior Explorers stacked adobe against the wall and by nine A.M. the new, deeper pits and trenches were ready for our next fire.

While the work crews had been busy, Julian continued checking weather conditions at thirty-minute intervals. Early morning today had been identical to the previous ones we had spent upon the desert. The sky was clear, winds were almost nonexistent and the temperature was just below 60 degrees. The sky began to brighten at four-forty-five and the sun burst over the mountains at five-sixteen.

By nine-thirty we had replenished the wood piles by the fire pit and left camp. We decided against leaving a guard at the site. In three days there we had seen no one, no lights, no tracks—no sign of life other than the lone condor that first morning. The midday heat was almost too much to ask anyone to sit through in the small supply tent we had set up beside the road.

After breakfast the launch crew readied the balloon, gondola, ballast and rigging for the drive out to the site. They had kept the braided weed lacings on the gondola moist by wiping them with a wet cloth twice daily. In Nazca's dry desert air we had noticed the gondola was lighter. Julian now needed the exact weight of everything—gondola, envelope, rope, ballast and crew.

When everything had been assembled in the parking compound, we rolled out the antique scale that the village grain merchant had lent us and were amazed to see Nazca's eternal dryness had already taken 22 pounds of moisture from our totora gondola. The reed boat that had registered 135 pounds at the airport in La Paz had now dehydrated to 113. The envelope and rigging weighed 485 and the crew 360.

With this total weight Julian was to project our flight plan. It was incongruous to see him sitting there astride the totora reed with a pocket calculator figuring how much heat we would need to lift our projected payload and how much ballast to ensure a safe descent. Our main question was how hot we could heat the smoky air inside the envelope and how fast and high Condor I would rise. The answers lay in the little red numbers that flashed across the calculator.

Julian took a considerable amount of gaff from the launch crew for using his post-Inca computer, but he always retorted that we were not going about this project by trial and error; and, after all, the final decision of how hot the balloon was would be one of judgment rather than calculation. We had no pyrometer in the Condor's crown, as modern balloons do, to tell the temperature.

After the gondola had been loaded in the truck with the balloon and the rigging ropes had been tested and weighed, we had a meeting to discuss an initial flight plan. Engineer Ken TeKrony joined Julian and me. The three of us had come to the point where we had to choose the way we thought best to fly.

Safety was our major consideration. We had brought parachutes for the two of us in case we planned to fly above 800 feet. We also felt the 45-pound chutes

163

could be used as ballast, if not in the conventional way.

"There are two aspects of this flight I think we can demonstrate," Julian said. "First, I think we'll be able to prove that smoke and native materials can be combined to carry two men off the plains. Second, I think we can show that this balloon, with a lesser weight—like the corpse of an Inca—could really climb high, just as Jay's paper models have done."

We all agreed it would be best to attempt an extended low-level flight—say to 500 or 600 feet—rather than a rapid high rise and rapid descent.

The two engineers talked to eventual agreement. Basically, they figured if we could raise the inside temperature of Condor I to 250 degrees on a morning when the outside temperature was no more than 60 degrees, the craft would carry the two-man crew and 400 pounds of ballast to 500 feet. The less the ballast, the more the altitude. A flight of 500 feet, they reasoned, would be a solid demonstration that "smoked" Peruvian textiles could have taken the heat and stress of flight. From the ground a flight to this height would be impressive—surely it would have seemed a great feat to early man.

With 150 pounds of weight in the gondola, we figured Condor I would go considerably higher. On a windless morning it would probably soar over 3,000 feet. Ken suggested that upon landing we should clear the balloon immediately, as it would most certainly rise very quickly if we had emptied it of all ballast on our descent.

As we talked over several other flight plans, the 500-foot flight seemed the safest and most convincing. That morning we made the decision not to wear parachutes and to trust the engineer's calculations.

"We'll meet tomorrow," Ken said. "Tonight we'll

inflate and smoke her well. We'll know more about expected lift then."

It was already noon. After lunch we turned in for the midday *siesta* along with the rest of Nazca. Our adobe-walled rooms were cool and quiet. Even the town's old rattling buses stopped in the midday heat. While out upon the *pampas*, our launching pad broiled under the persistent sun. I slept straight through until midnight. It was to be our last free afternoon.

13

One Hell of a Fire

"Happy Thanksgiving," Lisa said as she jostled me. "Julian asked me to wake you. He's worried about clouds over the eastern mountains."

I dressed quickly and went onto the patio, where Julian was talking with pilot Joe Pauley.

"It's the change of seasons," Joe was explaining. "There is never rain, but sometimes clouds and occasional gusts of wind crop up at odd hours. It seems early this year, but that's what those clouds are. You may not feel it, but there are subtle seasonal changes here in our desert climate."

"Don't worry," he said. "There shouldn't be any strong winds until late afternoon. That's when the steady breezes come and the *torremolinos* sweep the plains."

I looked into the sky and saw traces of white moon-lit clouds. There was absolutely no wind and the cool evening seemed like the four previous ones we'd experienced since arriving in Nazca. The keenness with which we now watched the weather was extraordinary. The impending flight and the anxiety it created within us aroused a new, unknown sensitivity to the touch of the wind and the look of the sky.

"Let's go," boomed Doc. "Load up the trucks and let's get smoking."

We now had a caravan heading out upon the desert.

169

The balloon and gondola filled our pickup truck and we hired a Jeep wagon to carry the Peruvian workers. Ten of our launch crew were packed into a Land-Rover.

The moon was still bright and the cloudscapes to the east had not spread as we unloaded Condor I. It was just after one when we slowly hauled the balloon's white shipping bag off the truck, and Doc marked off an area from which we would have to remove all rocks.

It was vital to clear the launch area of stones, because just laying out the fabric on the small football field in town during the painting and sewing had resulted in several small stones cutting nasty L-shaped scars into the fabric.

"I'm beginning to feel like an ancient Nazca," said Jay on his hands and knees in the moonlight as he picked rocks from the area around the balloon. Why didn't we just use one of their launch areas and save ourselves all this trouble?"

It took over an hour to clear away all the rocks we could see, and only then did Doc direct the crew to unroll the huge balloon. By two-thirty Condor I was flat and rigged for inflation. The giant condor Tommy had painted lay upon the desert looking up toward the sky.

"It's immense just lying there," Julian said as we walked around checking the half-inch rope lines that were fastened to the leather crown.

As we rigged the poles and checked the stakes, the pit crew began stoking a fire in the new deepened pit. The firelight, the bright moonlit sky and the great white balloon spread out before us made the scene an impressive one, and photographer Larry Gordon began recording the first steps of inflation.

At two-forty-five we checked the weather. It was holding perfectly. There was no wind and the smoke from the pit was curling straight skyward. It was time to begin smoking the giant.

Doc had run a ridge line from the two poles through the balloon's crown and now gave the signal to pull it tight. As it was tightened, the crown of the empty balloon rose to a point midway between the two poles. From the leather crown the top third of the balloon's fabric hung like a giant limp sack. Next Doc and Jim Winkler burrowed under the mountain of fabric still left upon the desert. Their job, with Les and Jimmy, was to drag the balloon's mouth over the smoke pit to make sure the smoke that began to rise would enter into Condor I.

This was the first moment all of us felt a new, uneasy respect for the immenseness of what we had built. Doc had warned of the dangers of smoke inhalation for anyone trapped within the thousands of square feet of fabric that lay piled upon the sand during the initial stages of inflation. We clearly saw the danger as the fabric closed over the smoke pit and as we watched the frail forms of four men burrowing deep inside. When they had the balloon's 52-foot-circumference mouth over the now-smoking pit, Doc and his helpers appeared out from under the fabric.

There was no noticeable effect for half an hour. There was no quick swelling of the envelope, as happens with a sport balloon when it's inflated with a quick burst of propane.

"Let her smoke," was all Doc said as he nervously circled the Condor I hanging limply from the ridge line.

In forty minutes there was a very small bulge just under the crown.

"That's the bubble," Doc said, standing beside me. "That's the answer to my prayer. We're beginning to trap smoke and hold a little hot air."

Earlier Doc had explained the basic principles of a smoke balloon. Almost any fabric with the strength to withstand the stress of flight can be used to construct a

171

smoke balloon. The cotton fabric we had selected, which matched the ancient Nazca grave fabric, was very porous and very heavy. Until the tiny smoke particles of a wood-burning fire would fill and clog these pores, the fabric would never fly.

"If we can smoke her five hours, you'll have one hell of a flight," Doc continued. "Look—that bubble's growing."

And it was. Now we all circled the balloon and slowly began helping the fabric unravel up and away from the ground.

On Doc's command we would slowly feed fabric toward the crown—a few inches at a time. Doc continuously circled the balloon, continuously checking the rise of the hot-air bubble, making sure the crown was level and that we were feeding fabric evenly on all sides.

By three-thirty Condor I had lifted a third of its fabric skyward. Smoke continued to curl inside the billowing envelope.

"Keep that fire roaring!" Doc bellowed.

John and Henry kept feeding large logs into the pit and pushing glowing charcoal stumps as far up into the tunnel as they could. The glow from the fire reached up through the tunnel into the smoke pit.

"That's one hell of a fire," Doc kept saying in his endless rounds around the growing, glowing balloon.

I was holding on beside Jim Winkler and Lisa. We had been there nearly two hours and had felt the cool, limp fabric first become warm, then almost hot as the smoke continued to swirl inside. We could press our faces against the fabric and smell the smoke that was escaping through the still-very-porous cloth.

When the balloon was half filled, Doc gave the command to cut away the poles.

"Cut away one!" he ordered, and Mike cut the center line and watched the giant pole fall instantly toward his stake. It fell onto the desert with a crash.

"Number two!" Doc shouted, and Les cut away the center line holding the second pole, and as it crashed down, Condor I stood on its own for the first time. It was now about the size of a four-story building and was visibly smoking from the top. The three designs began to show—the condor, the spiral and the eyes of the sun god were now peeking over the rolls of fabric still to rise.

"Marvelous!" Julian's excited English accent exclaimed. "It's marvelous."

He had stopped for a moment in the back, where I was alternately looking for sparks and feeding fabric toward the crown. We agreed that the inflation was right on schedule. The fabric was smoking well and the bubble was now growing even faster than we had hoped.

Each of us holding the fabric was now alone. The heat had puffed the balloon to such a size that we all separated, and each of us seemed to fit into his own small fold in the billowing fabric. Doc had asked us to keep the rising balloon tight against the bubble, and when the lift began to tug we were to feed a little fabric at a time toward the top. In the process the rising, expanding fabric had cut us off from each other's sight.

I was standing there alone astonished at the balloon's growing lift when I first saw the smoke. To my right a thin line of smoke was escaping out between the fabric and the sand. For a moment I was too puzzled to react. Then I yelled to Jim Winkler, whom I knew was holding near me.

"Smoke!" I screamed. "It's underneath the balloon!"

Jim instantly began burrowing under the hundreds of feet of fabric to open a tunnel toward the smoking pit. I struggled in behind him holding the heavy fabric above my head.

173

The smoke was thick, hot, black and impossible to breathe. When I lifted a final fold of cloth, I was astonished to suddenly see the smoke pit just before me. In it were flames, but I couldn't see what was burning.

I held the heavy fabric above us both, and in the black-orange light I saw another form frantically throwing sand into the pit. It was Julian, who had heard our screams and had also burrowed in toward the smoke pit.

The three of us were barely aware of each other, and as we kicked sand madly to stop the fire there was suddenly a flash of light and a rush of fresh air where we stood. Doc and the pit crew had rolled back a wall of fabric to reach us at the smoke pit. Buckets of sand were thrown in the pit and the smoldering stopped. We gulped the fresh, cool air.

Above us Condor I stood a good six stories high, and its huge mass of hot, smoky air held it from dropping upon us. I could feel the smoke burn in my chest.

"It was the rigging," Julian said as he dug down into the still-smoking sand.

The 20-foot lines that would link the gondola to the balloon had somehow fallen into the smoke pit and the heat had been so intense they had ignited. We pulled charred rope bits from the sand and inspected the mouth of the still-towering balloon. The balloon was untouched, but new gondola lines would have to be rigged.

"Dig out the smoke pit," Doc ordered. "And dig it out fast—we're losing inflation."

The Junior Explorers feverishly cleared the smoke pit of the sand we'd kicked in to suffocate the rope fire. With each shovel lifted out of the pit, new smoke would begin curling upward. Soon the pit was clear and Doc ordered the Condor's mouth to be carefully slid back over the pit.

174

"Stoke her up!" he yelled, and new wood was instantly laid on the dwindling fire.

When I stepped back from the pit, I saw how badly the balloon was sagging. She had lost half of the inflation we had achieved and seemed to be sinking fast.

"She'll fill faster this time," Doc said. "Keep pouring that smoke in. The more we smoke her, the easier she'll be to inflate. Stoke her up!"

He was right. Within ten minutes we had the giant back to the height she was before the rope fire. Smoke now billowed into the mouth of the great balloon. The crown was holding and building up a heavy concentration of smoke particles. The balloon began to rise dramatically. Suddenly, surprisingly, the moment quickly came when she was nearly full. Holding and feeding up the last fabric folds, I could feel a new strong tug on our hands. Condor I was filled with smoke and hot air and getting hotter.

"Ease off on the fire," Doc ordered, and John and Henry raked back some of the coals from inside the tunnel. Earlier Doc had explained that from this point on we should reduce the heat but continue smoking, or "curing" the balloon.

Now, as the fire was being raked back, all seventeen of us held tightly onto the mammoth balloon. It was like trying to stand around a ten-story building that kept tugging skyward. Our fingers began to ache as Doc and the Peruvian work crew circled the mouth and staked the remaining lines to the ground.

As engineer Ken TeKrony stood beside me helping to hold the giant down, he smiled and said simply, "She'll fly."

Within fifteen minutes the fire was well under control. Condor I was staked around the mouth as thick smoke continued to curl up inside its towering envelope. It was the first time we could step back and see what we had created. The sight was overwhelming! I

175

walked back fifty yards to take it all in and couldn't believe how majestic the balloon had become. There— over ten stories above the sand, glowing from within by the soft light of the fire, lit by the moon and decorated with designs from the desert—was our magnificent airship. It was a thrill I shall never forget. For several minutes most of us just admired the great balloon and watched the smoke rising within it.

The first light of dawn was slowly edging onto the horizon, and with it came a soft, unexpected rustle of wind. Since we had come to the plains there had been occasional light wind during pre-dawn hours. So, when the first slight rustle began, we were unconcerned and kept flooding smoke up inside Condor I.

At five o'clock the sky was bright and the sun was beginning to backlight the edges of the far eastern mountains. Then suddenly with the light came the first strong gust of wind. In an instant it caught the spiral side of Condor I and our giant balloon suddenly became a mammoth sail.

We had moored the three 120-foot-long crown lines to a parked truck and Land-Rovers, and we had double-staked the sixteen lower lines around the fire pit area. Additionally, seventeen men were assigned positions on the holding rope we had sewn around the balloon's 52-foot mouth. With the first strong gust, the holding lines on two Land-Rovers snapped with a sharp crack.

Instantly Doc ordered the holding crew to hang on to the balloon's mouth. He shouted to Jay to slash the remaining crown line.

I saw that the wind was gusting to thirteen miles per hour on our anemometer, and by the time Jay reached the Land-Rover, Condor I had pulled it several feet across the sand. Just before the final crown line was cut, the balloon arched with the wind and all of us holding the mouth felt our feet becoming light in the sand.

The one rule we had carefully explained to everyone was that the moment your feet left the ground you were to let go immediately. The balloon could rise as much as 15 to 20 feet per second, and a two- or three-second delay could leave a man dangling more than 50 feet in the air and rising rapidly with a runaway balloon. The one other precaution that had been drilled into everyone in both English and Spanish was to avoid any entanglement in the ropes and rigging. We didn't want anyone taken aloft entwined and dangling in a line.

As the wind gusted against the balloon, we clung to the holding rope and felt ourselves being pulled slowly along the sandy desert with the swaying monster. The power of the smoke and heat we had captured inside the great bag was terrifying. As we clung on desperately, Doc and three of the Peruvians were struggling to point one of the ear lines into the wind.

"Pull her down!" ordered Doc. "Pull her down!"

Four men tugged on the tetrahedron's ear and swung it low and into the wind. Condor I seemed to twist as they pulled, and as the wind continued gusting I could feel the fabric sag in my hands. The balloon was cooling rapidly. Instead of rising, it now began to flap wildly.

"Don't let the fabric fall on you!" shouted Julian as he raced beside those of us attempting to hold the mouth down.

Condor I was filled with 80,000 cubic feet of thick black smoky air, and anyone trapped under a sagging pile of fabric would suffocate quickly. It was like holding on to a collapsing building. I could feel the heat escaping from the mouth as the wind relentlessly pushed the balloon across the sand.

As most of us were being dragged along, Doc had

managed to get four more men on another ear line, and when they had pulled it low and into the wind, Doc ordered those of us on the mouth to let go.

"Let the mouth go!" he shouted. "Release it!"

With a loud snap the mouth flew from our hands and went with the wind. We watched it flap 50 feet above us and then begin belching smoke as the ear lines held and gusting wind quickly helped deflate the giant bag.

Within a minute over two hours' worth of smoke had gushed out of Condor I. We watched it trail out across the *pampas*. As the fabric began falling, several of us raced to help hold the ear lines into the wind.

Soon the empty balloon was on the sand. It had blown over 80 yards from the smoking pit before we had released the mouth. Almost the moment it touched the desert floor the wind died. The last sudden gust had expelled most of the smoke. Now the balloon was no more than a great white spot on the desert, and calm had returned to Nazca. We watched the dark smoke cloud the balloon had expelled slowly vanish in the bright morning sky.

Doc and Julian were already burrowing inside the mouth to check the fabric. I tunneled in after them and saw Doc's big smile as he examined the inside of the balloon. A thin gray color covered the fabric.

"Look at that," he said proudly. "Look at that curing."

Doc had been convinced the fabric would "cure" well, and the gray color was convincing. The cotton was trapping smoke particles, and with further smoking the balloon would surely become as non-porous as a modern-day nylon balloon.

"This will take you up," he added. "You'll fly plenty high on this gray. Up near the crown I'll bet it's nearly black already. The fire is sealing the fabric beautifully."

We rolled the balloon into a giant 80-foot snake where it had fallen. Next we cleared a wide trail of rocks and stones back to the fire pit. It took twenty of us half an hour to carefully drag Condor I back to the inflation pit. We all had a new respect for the balloon's inflated power—it was a monster.

Now the wind had died completely and the sun was rising fast. We extinguished the pit fire and checked the tunnel for hot spots that we had feared might cause another collapse, but the fire and the tunnel had worked perfectly. Only the wind had been our enemy this night.

We left a four-man detail at the site to clean out the fire pit and restack new firewood. The rest of us piled into the vehicles for the drive back to breakfast.

"We'll need stronger rope on the crown lines," Doc advised as we drove. "The quarter-inch lines snapped the moment the first gust hit. We'll need at least half-inch lines everywhere to ride out anything like that again."

"We should be prepared for the same thing again," Julian added. "Joe Pauley said gusts are unusual, but not to be surprised if we get another."

"We'll devise a plan to ride out the gusts," Doc said. "Condor I has a very large surface in relation to her volume—but I'm sure we can stake her down well as we smoke and keep the ear lines ready to head into the wind. We're fliers, not sailors—but we damned well better be able to come about if we have to."

After full plates of grilled beefsteak, eggs and steaming cups of hot *milo,* we all slept until mid-afternoon. Then I bought 1,200 feet of three-quarter-inch rope and Doc braided in the eyes and knots that would secure them to the crown. We fashioned twenty-five new 3-foot stakes from 2-by-2 hardwood beams.

"We can ride out a gust of up to twenty miles per hour if we stake and tie her right," Doc said convincingly. "And tomorrow we'll stake her well the moment she's inflated."

We drove back to the hotel with the heavier rope and larger stakes filling the back of the pickup. Lisa was at the front door to remind us Thanksgiving dinner was ready. We hurried inside and celebrated with Nazca's traditional fiesta meal—curried goat. It was hot, savory and delicious. We washed it down with cold liters of beer and fell into bed ready for the midnight call—and hopefully the flight of Condor I.

14

Get Ready to Fly

"PERFECT!" WAS JULIAN'S VERDICT AS WE looked into the midnight sky above the hotel's garden patio. The sweeping old Bougainvillaea that climbed above the roof was motionless. There was not a whisper of wind in the cool air. The sky was brilliantly clear and all the thousands of stars one never sees in the cities were there above us.

"A perfect night to fly," Julian continued. "I can't believe it's going so well."

"You mean, despite burning up the rigging and being dragged across the *pampas* last night, everything looks okay," John chided.

"I mean, here it is—the day we planned to fly— and Doc says another three hours of smoking and we'll be ready," Julian answered. "I'd say we're right on schedule."

And we were. The convoy of trucks that took us out onto the plains was now joined by dozens of vehicles—battered old taxis from Nazca, some slick new cars with the press corps down from Lima, TV camera crews in stake trucks and some rattling old buses that were to get permanently stuck at the archeological zone entrance. It was a far cry from the lone Land-Rover we had driven out upon the plains just six nights ago when we had selected the launch site. Suddenly, here in the middle of the desolate Nazca plains, at a few minutes past midnight, nearly one thousand people were driving out upon the desert.

"Bet this hasn't happened for at least fifteen hundred years," Jay commented. Earlier at dinner, over the curried goat, he had presented several unique theories on how the large Nazca trapezoids had been ceremonial inflation areas for tetrahedron airships.

"I should have come in costume," Jay added. "I feel I'm not really dressed for this event in Levi's. We should have made ceremonial robes, or at least worn some of the ones the grave robbers find."

"The skull at the site is enough for me," Doc said. "Let's get Condor up, and then I'll buy you any poncho you want in Lima."

When we arrived at the site, the Junior Explorers had already started the fire. A glowing bed of coals was smoking in the deep pit. The balloon had been unrolled and the giant condor design was vivid in the fire and moonlight.

"Everything's ready here," the youngsters reported to Doc. "Wind is zero, fire is ready and the balloon has been patched."

In the late afternoon Lisa and Lucia had checked the fabric for burn holes from the rigging fire and for small L-shaped tears caused by rocks. They had sewn over twenty-five small patches, mainly near the mouth.

At one A.M. the launch crew was gathered around Doc for a final briefing. He covered the inflation and smoking procedures and then went over the gondola assembly with Ken and Jay. Doc's orders were translated for the Peruvian crew and by one-fifteen we were ready to begin inflation.

The fire's bed was pushed up into the mouth of the tunnel and fresh timber was piled high upon the glowing coals. A thick blue column of smoke appeared instantly and was clearly visible even in the darkness.

On Doc's command the line crew pulled the ridge rope taut and Condor I's crown rose 40 feet above the *pampas*. Next the holding crew moved the mouth over the smoke pit and shoved the loose fabric piles into position. The column of smoke disappeared into the mouth of the inert balloon.

Inflation was almost instantaneous. The already-smoked fabric held the fire's heat and Doc's "bubble" appeared instantly. We could visibly watch the hot air fill the crown and the lifeless balloon began to stir within minutes. Doc and Julian kept circling the balloon and advising to let out a little fabric here, hold tight there, feed a little to the crown, hold tight. The balloon grew quickly on all sides. Within fifteen minutes Condor I was nearly one-third inflated. It all seemed very easy—almost routine.

Then, inexplicably, the crown began to slip. We had been feeding the fabric slowly up as the hot air tugged it skyward, but somehow the smoke had worked into one of the massive tetrahedron's ears, and suddenly our inflation was becoming lopsided. Four men were ordered to pull the ear down, but it was too late. The thousands of cubic feet of smoke that had gathered there had far more strength than we could muster on a single line.

The next half hour was a grim wrestling match. First Doc would order men to hold firm on one side and others would feed loose cloth up toward the crown. But that didn't work—the ear only dragged more fabric dangerously near the fire pit. At one point, half the twisted balloon hovered 30 feet above the fire and we were terrified any sudden, unexplained wind might dip Condor I onto the open flames. Our wood was so dry that we had long ago quit worrying about sparks, but the new twisting inflation was an unexpected hazard. We could not seem to force a straight inflation, and the monster kept leaning closer to the desert floor.

"Cut the smoke," Doc reluctantly ordered, and the

boys immediately placed a barricade at the end of the tunnel to cut the smoky hot air from rising into the balloon.

"Let her cool!" Doc shouted.

The night air was brisk and when the hot smoke was cut from the Condor's mouth, the balloon began to sag quickly. Within a few minutes the tug was gone for those holding the fabric and soon one could feel the balloon begin to sag and sink.

"Reel her in and pile it at your feet!" Doc shouted as he circled the rapidly deflating balloon.

When the crown had dropped even with the ridge rope, the holders on the backside hauled in mountains of loose cloth. Finally, when the piles of fabric seemed even all around, Doc ordered the smoke pit opened again. When the heat began flowing again, Julian burrowed inside to make sure no rigging lines or cloth had slipped into the smoke pit.

Almost immediately inflation was well under way again. Now, with the fabric even more smoked than before, the bubble formed quickly and the balloon rose visibly. Within fifteen minutes she was a third full and seemed to be growing straight toward the sky— and with the three ears filling evenly.

"Hold that fabric tight," Doc and Julian ordered as they circled the inflating balloon.

"*Aguantalo fuertementa*," we said, translating for the Peruvians holding alongside.

By three A.M. the balloon had filled to the point where its drawings were all visible and well off the ground. Now more than thirty men held the remaining fabric. Each hand gripped several folds at a time, for the thin cotton would tear easily if a single thickness was tugged with too much force. Doc gave the order for the poles to be cut away and they fell with a crack onto the sand.

I looked down at the diminishing pile of cloth at

my feet. We were nearing complete inflation, and within minutes the heavy rope holding ring sewn just above the balloon's mouth slipped up into our grip. Condor I was filled with 80,000 cubic feet of hot, smoky air and beginning to tug at her lines.

At three-fifteen Doc ordered the fire banked. The hottest coals were raked back from inside the adobe tunnel and new logs were placed on them. A steady stream of smoke was drawn up into the inclining tunnel. Our plan was to smoke the balloon until dawn, then fire up, cut her loose and fly.

There was not a whisper of wind or a cloud. Doc and the launch crew were busy double-staking the mooring lines around the mouth to the new 2-by-2 stakes we had cut during the afternoon.

When the fully inflated balloon was well staked at the mouth, tied to three trucks and held tightly by the ear lines, we all relaxed for the first time since we had been on the desert that night.

Condor I was up straight and firm. Thick, dark blue smoke continued to billow up from the pit into the balloon. The fire pit crew now had fine control over the heat—they were putting out a thick smoke with as little heat as possible directed into the balloon. Condor I was near equilibrium and resting nicely. We had only to continue smoking, sealing the tiny pores in the cotton, and to wait for dawn. It was time to prepare the gondola for flight.

Julian and I carried our reed boat into the light of the fire to check its lines. We would be suspended from two load points by twin 5,000-pound-test manila ropes that had been woven into the reed. These would be tied on to four main lines formed from the crown support ropes that ran down through the balloon. Also above the gondola were two half-inch lines that were to be our safety belts should the reed boat fail. On takeoff we would cinch the safety lines around our waists with a snug slipknot that could be quickly untied for landing. We had practiced this procedure many times.

We went over the final launch instructions with Doc, Ken, Jay and Lisa. Julian would tie the joining knots, I would secure and place the ballast and Ken and Jay would keep the mouth and balloon in the right position. Lisa would be in charge of instruments. We had walked through the procedure many times, tied the securing and safety knots, boarded the ballast-laden boat in our flight suits and helmets and snapped on our altimeters and variometer. It was a familiar routine.

"When we get ready to go, there won't be much time," Doc had continually cautioned. "We'll bring the gondola in under the mouth, secure the lines, board the crew and cut her loose within a minute."

Speed was necessary because of the smoke. Even if we sealed off the fire pit, the heavy concentration of smoke inside the balloon would curl out of its mouth. The area directly under the mouth was very smoky and Ken, who had already spent considerable time under there checking for fire, was very hoarse. His face was already as black as a coal miner's at the end of a long, hard shift.

We continued reviewing the launch. Once Julian and I were aboard, the 20-foot lines between the gondola and the balloon would be fed up slowly as the super-heated balloon was maintained in equilibrium. When the lines were taut, Doc would give the command to cut the balloon free from all outside lines. We would then be free and our rise would be immediate and estimated at 15 to 18 feet per second. It would be a fast ride up.

Julian and I went over to the Land-Rover and slipped into our flight uniforms—U.S. Navy fire-resistant coveralls and crash helmets. Lisa had the instruments and we checked them. Julian would wear the variometer on a line around his neck. The instrument's face was visible to us both, and it clearly showed the rate of ascent or descent in large white numbers against the black dial. On our right thighs we would clip the altimeters.

We continued nervously checking the gondola and our equipment. We reweighed the eight 50-pound sacks of ballast and checked their release knots. Julian rechecked all knots that would secure us and the gondola to the balloon. Everything was set. We were smoking and it was an hour before dawn.

At four the weather check was perfect—no wind, and a temperature of 58 degrees. The sky was perfectly cloudless. At five-fifteen there was no change. Then, just before five-thirty, when Julian was getting ready to log that reading, the needle on the anemometer signaled trouble. A ripple of wind suddenly bounced the needle to six miles per hour.

"Wind!" Julian yelled to Doc, who was standing before the fire watching the smoke funneling down the trench toward Condor I.

Instantly Doc ran to the most southerly ear line shouting for help. Four men were there instantly and they all began pulling the ear low and into the direction Julian was pointing.

The wind came fast. This time it was not a gust but a steady rush that was cool to our faces and seemed to come straight from the high mountains to the south. The impact upon the Condor was immediate.

The giant balloon caved in at the middle. For an instant I stood frozen at the weather station watching the huge envelope buckle. I was afraid the balloon might be torn away. Condor I was very near equilibrium when the wind hit. If she ripped loose now with no crew or ballast, the giant would surely climb over 3,000 feet. This was going to be our most severe test.

189

Instantly the wind stoked the fire white-hot and searing smoke and cinders rushed into the tunnel. The mouth of the balloon glowed with the fire's increased flames.

"Hang on!" shouted Julian and Doc as they stood, backs to the wind, directing the line crews to hold. "Hang on all lines and hold tight on the mouth!"

"Guardalo bien, guardalo fuerte!"

Now the balloon was tugging at the stakes and at our aching fingers. Beside me, newspapermen were helping hold the fabric, and near the mouth I saw Maria Reiche, who had come to observe, holding tightly onto a rope beside our crew. The wind was steady and Condor I had now become a giant sail being held taut against it.

"Fire!" shouted a frantic voice behind the balloon. *"Fuego! Fuego!"*

A large cinder had struck near the holding ring and was searing a gaping hole in the fabric. By the time Ken had covered it with sand, it had burned a watermelon-sized hole just above the mouth. Lucia was there immediately with fabric and needle to patch the opening. Several other sparks seemed to fly against the fabric, and wherever they did someone was there to stamp it out or cover the burn with sand.

As the wind continued the stronger half-inch lines were holding. Doc had two ears pulled low and pointing into the wind. None of the cars had been dragged, nor had the Condor's mouth been pulled off the smoking pit.

The wind blew another five minutes. On the anemometer it gusted to fourteen miles per hour, and still we held. There was smoke and dust and sand swirling around the pit, and sparks stopped flying when Doc had the coals covered with a windbreaker. We held on and the great sail above us kept tugging to fly.

The balloon had now been smoked so well that it

held the hot air far longer than the night before. After five minutes of strong wind the balloon was still firm and tugging at the stakes. Heat and smoke still flowed up through the tunnel, but the glow of the covered fire was gone.

Then, as quickly as the wind had come, it vanished. When it suddenly stopped, the great balloon sagged slightly and the crown lines looped toward the ground. Condor I was beginning to cool.

"Dig out those coals," Doc ordered, and the pit boys raked hot embers up out of the sand. New kindling was thrown on and instantly the thick shavings burst into flame. The fire was back within minutes, and smoke and heat again began pouring out of the pit. The Condor responded at once. She was now a true hot-air balloon. As the fire roared and the smoke billowed, Doc turned to me as the first light of dawn was in the sky.

"Get ready to fly," he said.

15

The Flight
of Condor I

THE SUN WAS RISING JUST BEHIND THE MOUN-tain peaks as we carried the gondola in under the mouth of Condor I. We had originally planned to fly at dawn, and it now looked as if we might make just that moment.

The wind had vanished. The anemometer reading was zero, and the red-and-white Peruvian streamers on the balloon's ears hung limply in the stillness.

"Now's the time," Julian said as we set the gondola down gently in the sand. "We're a few minutes from sunrise and the weather is perfect."

Inside the huge balloon's mouth there was feverish activity. The scene was lit by an orange glow from the smoke pit. Doc had ordered the fire stoked to its limit, and smoke and light poured into the mouth of Con-dor I. Our plan was to raise the balloon to equilibrium, connect the gondola, then quickly super-heat her to the fabric's limit until we could hold her no more.

Jay and Ken were checking the rigging that tied the envelope to the gondola. Henry was watching the smoke flow for sparks. I was loading the ballast bags in the center of the gondola. Doc and a three-man crew were busy slashing the staked lines. Over thirty men and Maria Reiche held down the balloon's mouth.

Within two minutes the staked lines were cut and the balloon was solely in the hands of the crew that ringed the mouth gripping the rope holding ring. The fire continued to pump smoke and heat up into the mouth as the gondola was rigged securely to the towering balloon. Four hundred pounds of ballast were aboard.

Condor I was plainly ready to fly. The ground crew continued holding her down with great effort. The fire continued billowing heat and smoke upward. At a signal from Doc, Julian and I mounted the gondola. We sat opposite each other with the ballast between. We slipped the safety harness ropes loosely around us and snapped on our crash helmets. Our added weight visibly nestled the gondola snugly into the sand. Heat and smoke kept pouring in.

We sat there for a full minute with the smoke swirling around us. More and more I could feel the balloon straining to rise. All around us in the orange light I saw the crew holding the mouth down. Above us there was only the dark cloud of smoke that filled the huge balloon.

Orders for the holders to free themselves of all lines were shouted in English and Spanish. Then Doc directed four men to hold each gondola support line.

"Release the holding ring," Doc ordered, and his command was echoed in Spanish.

The balloon was now resting on the four gondola lines, and the sixteen strongest men we had were fighting to keep them down.

"Play out the lines!" Doc shouted.

The four lines were allowed to slowly slip up and the balloon's mouth began to rise away from the smoke pit.

"Let her go!" Doc shouted.

I felt a sharp tug and suddenly realized that Condor I was flying. I quickly cinched the safety slipknot around my waist and looked down. I was astonished!

196

We were over 50 feet high and climbing rapidly away from the ring of our crewmen below. Up we went in the dawn light with an enormous shout from below.

"Eighteen feet per second!" Julian shouted as we rose quickly and silently up above the plains. In those first few seconds we could hardly comprehend our rapid ascent. Liftoff had been incredibly smooth. All our worries about stress and snapped rigging had been for naught. The liftoff had been flawless, and now we climbed swiftly up and away from the smoke and noise of the launch pit.

"Two hundred fifty," Julian counted off as he checked his altimeter. "Now climbing at 12 feet per second. I hope we haven't overdone it."

The rapid rise continued for several more seconds until our rate of climb slowed sharply. As we climbed I checked all lines, safety knots, balance and ballast —everything was perfect. We were riding evenly astride our reed boat and dangling nearly 30 feet below the balloon. I looked up into the black, smoky mouth of Condor I and saw a few small burn holes we had missed patching near the holding ring.

We climbed for forty-five seconds before beginning to level off. It felt like an elevator arriving at the top floor after a long ride up. We seemed to surge upward for a moment, then settle back. When I looked over the edge of our reed boat, we were dangling nearly 400 feet above the desert. The view was spectacular.

The sun had just cleared the mountains and now flooded the fantastic scene below. As we hung there drifting slightly to the northwest, I was astonished to see a long Nazca runway perhaps 300 yards off our starboard side. It was possibly a coincidence, but what a coincidence!

We shouted to each other to look at the long, fantastic runway. To our left we could see long, straight lines running away to the horizon. Behind us the launch area now seemed far away, and the people and cars seemed very small and detached from our new world. From our dangling perch our Condor also seemed small. Above us we could see only the mouth and part of the huge smoky cloud it held. Nazca, however, was immense and spread out gloriously below.

For the next two minutes the balloon held an even course and we became sightseers. The liftoff had been so incredibly smooth and the climb to 380 feet so rapid that all our nervousness suddenly changed to exhilaration.

The great plains ran to the horizon and several ancient lines stood out clearly in the morning sun. Surely, I thought, the men who created these lines had to have seen them like this—with the shadows of dawn etching their magnificent art.

For those two minutes we were there alone with Nazca. We had flown back in time as much as we had climbed into the sky. We were riding the wind and following the ancient lines in the early light of the sun. There was no sound there, no jet roar, no rush of wind from our wings. We were there with the elements of the *pampas,* riding along like a pair of trespassers from the twentieth century. It was a highly emotional experience to fly in our fire-powered chariot, above those great, ancient lines, powered by the wind and held by a giant cloud of smoke. At three minutes into the flight our altitude was holding. We could feel, however, that Condor I was beginning to descend.

The variometer registered a slow 10-foot-per-minute drop, and then it suddenly jumped to 25. As we felt the fall, we let her slip away to 300 feet before jettisoning two sacks of ballast. The 100 pounds slowed the descent almost instantly, and we leveled off for several seconds before again beginning to plummet, this time to 30 feet per minute. We dropped to 200 feet quickly and shoved out 200 pounds of sand. The effect was immediate—we leveled off almost instantly.

We held at 180 feet for half a minute before beginning to slide again toward the desert. Our descent was a comfortable 20 feet per minute, and when we reached an altitude of 80 feet Julian signaled to jettison the next to last sack of ballast. I let the sand fall away as I watched the *pampas* seemingly come up straight toward us.

"Fifty!" Julian shouted. "Thirty!" We both unfastened our safety lines.

"Ten!"

We bumped onto the sandy plain. A cloud of dust kicked up where we hit, but the reed cushioned the shock of what little vertical speed we had.

"Jump clear," Julian commanded, and we both leaped from the gondola onto the sand. The moment we were clear Condor I instantly rose above us. The ballooon, now free of our 360 pounds, shot skyward with great acceleration.

"My God!" Julian cried. "There goes your journey to the sun!"

We watched the great balloon rise straight above us to over 1,200 feet and sail away with a high wind to the northwest. Condor I turned slowly as she flew —first the spiral, then the condor and finally the sun god would shine above us in the sunlight.

"Do you know how high we could send a lightweight Inca corpse with that balloon?" Julian thought aloud. "We could send it easily over 5,000 feet. Then if we dyed the fabric black and launched her at midday, solar energy would take it out of sight."

"Now do you think the god Viracocha could have flown back to the sun, as the legends say?" I asked.

"Well, we've proved to my satisfaction that he could have," Julian answered. "You know, up there just now I had the feeling we weren't the first ever to

199

have flown with the wind above Nazca. Did you sense it?"

Before I could answer a horde of ground crew and press were upon us. John and Doc had run all the way from the launch area—well over a mile away—and they were brandishing a bottle of French champagne.

"To the Montgolfiers!" John shouted as he uncorked the traditional post-flight ballooning beverage and splashed it upon all of us.

High above, Condor I still sailed with the wind. While we were surrounded by noisy well-wishers, we strained to follow the path of the great balloon. She drifted easily with the wind and now was holding at about 1,000 feet several miles away.

"She's so well smoked that she'll fly a long time," Doc said. "When you took off she had to be well above 250 degrees at the crown. With only the gondola as payload, she'll drift for miles."

The sun was now very bright and Condor I's red spiral stood out vividly against the sky as she slowly descended.

"We left one sack of ballast aboard," I told Doc.

"It's a good thing neither of you is aboard," he answered. "A 180-pound man up there 1,000 feet with only 50 pounds of ballast would have one hell of a fast ride down."

We thought of how the Inca legends told of young boys who were sent aloft to observe. I wondered how long it had taken them to understand the use of ballast. There surely had been tragic experimental flights when those first pilots learned to conquer the sky with fire, smoke and sand.

Condor I was descending now—a graceful symbol slowly sliding earthward with its tiny crescent gondola suspended there inviting us to ride again.

Julian and I watched her strike the desert several miles away. She dragged for a minute before a large puff of black smoke belched out into the sky and the balloon crumpled below the horizon. The flight of Condor I had ended. She had flown for fourteen minutes.

Maria Reiche shook both our hands and then led a group out across her *pampas* to where the balloon had finally fallen. Her sturdy seventy-two-year-old legs, which had walked the *pampas* for twenty-seven years, beat all others to the fallen balloon.

When Julian and I arrived there, we checked the gondola and rigging. The lines were all fast and the totora reed had stood up well to the impact of both landings. The balloon was intact and lay undamaged upon the sand.

Later that morning we dismantled the launch site and trucked all we had hauled out upon the plains back to town. Julian and I left in the last Land-Rover, and during that final long drive across the *pampas* we seldom spoke. Our thoughts were still on the moments we had just spent over Nazca.

Later that morning I received instructions from the Peruvian government to pack the balloon and gondola for shipment to the capital. Condor I was destined for the National Aeronautical Museum in Lima.

As we packed that marvelous balloon for the final time, I was asked by the press to evaluate our adventure. To answer them I went back to the original legends that had drawn us to Nazca. I retold the story of Imaymana Viracocha ("The Maker"), which says "he ascended into the sky after having finished making all that there is in the land."

I believe that is what happened. Nazca was not an ancient landing field—it was just the oppsite. The lines, burn pits and "runways" were once takeoff sites for a religion that worshipped the sun. Our flight was a modern demonstration of an ancient religious ceremony. With what we have learned we could now easily build a large balloon of Nazca textiles, dye it black,

201

and then the solar gain of the midday sun would take a man—or a corpse—up out of sight on an apparent "journey to the sun."

After our flight above that great ritual stage, I now have tremendous admiration for "primitive" man. It is time we honor these daring, ingenious men who lived on the frontiers of our civilization. To attempt to explain away their colossal achievements by crediting people from other planets is blasphemy.

EPILOGUE

ON OUR FINAL DAY IN NAZCA, THE MAYORS OF
Nazca's surrounding towns pledged adequate funds
to provide twenty-four-hour patrol protection of the
Archeological Zone along the Pan American High-
way. To avoid bureaucratic entanglement they named
Maria Reiche to administer the fund. The original
$1,000 donation of the International Explorers So-
ciety had successfully started the drive to save the
Nazca lines. The campaign to protect Nazca continues.
Readers interested in this and similar Explorer proj-
ects may contact the society by writing: International
Explorers, 3132 Ponce de Leon Boulevard, Coral
Gables, Miami, Florida 33134.

Keep Up With The BESTSELLERS!

Keep Up With The BEST SELLERS!